Y0-DKN-778

KINDLE FREE FOR ALL:

How to Get Millions of Free Kindle Books and Other

Free Content With or Without an Amazon Kindle

For Use with the Latest Generation Kindle 3G, Kindle

Wi-Fi, Kindle DX, and Kindle Apps

(Prices Apply to US Kindle Customers, But Much Free

Content Linked Herein Can Be Downloaded

Anywhere)

By Stephen Windwalker

Kindle Nation Daily

KINDLE FREE FOR ALL:

How to Get Millions of Free Kindle Books and Other Free Content With or Without an Amazon Kindle

By Stephen Windwalker

Print Edition Published by Windwalker Media

kindlenation@gmail.com

Arlington, Massachusetts

Visit Kindle Nation Daily at http://www.kindlenationdaily.com

For readers everywhere, and the authors who feed us

Table of Contents

Editor's Note

Throughout this book, you will find references to various websites, as well as to specific items on Amazon and other websites. For the reader's convenience and ease of use, lengthy and non-intuitive web addresses have been provided in the form of shortened hyperlinks. The shortened links will be much easier to manually copy while typing into a browser window, but they must be typed exactly as they appear, as they are case-sensitive.

A clickable list of all the links in this book, listed in order by chapter, has also been made available at the Kindle Nation Daily website, here: http://bit.ly/FFA-links .

Preface: How To Use This Book

Thank you for buying my book, Kindle Free for All. And don't worry, I'm not going to insult you by providing a manual on how to use what is, essentially, a manual.

But one thing. Now if you purchase the Kindle version of this book, you will be free to download it to an unlimited number of your Kindle-registered devices, and I want to suggest that you will be able to get the most out of it if you

keep a copy with your Kindle for PC or Kindle for Mac app. That will allow you to move seamlessly between the text and the web pages to which I provide links throughout the text in that version. However, those links are also provided here in the text of this hard copy edition, as well as in a handy list at http://www.kindlenationdaily.com.

For any book you have purchased in the Kindle Store, it's a snap to have Amazon send a copy to your other devices.

1

Just use your computer to go to your Manage Your Kindle page (http://amzn.to/KFFA1) and scroll down to "Your Orders." Find this title and use the "Deliver to" pulldown menu to select your device. Within a few seconds you should hear the sizzle of wires burning and the book will appear on the Home screen of the Kindle app to which you have sent it.

Okay, one other thing. I do want to apologize for the fact that, contrary to the overblown claim implicit in the title of this book, some of the free books mentioned are free only in Amazon's U.S.-based Kindle store, and then only for countries where various taxes, duties, and fees have not been added. However, much of the other web-based free content is free throughout the universe.

Ch 1: How Can This Be? Amazon May Be Making Billions, But Kindle is the Key to "Free"

Getting Started

Welcome to the world of the amazing Amazon Kindle. It's that *expensive* ebook reader you've been hearing about, or ... maybe you just grabbed yours from under the tree and opened it up for the first time?

Expensive? Well, the earliest Kindle models *did* cost $399 to $489, but out of respect for the possibility that someone you love may have just given you yours, we won't make a big deal of the fact that the price has now come all the way down to the $139-$189 range (and sometimes lower for refurbished, earlier-generation models). Or $379 for the considerably larger Kindle DX with the 9.7-inch display.

Or FREE, if you are -- for now -- skipping the Kindle device itself altogether and downloading a free Kindle App for your iPad, iPhone, iPod Touch, Android device, BlackBerry, PC, or Mac or using the new "Kindle for the Web" browser.

(For your convenience, we will include a section here on how to download these free Kindle Apps for other devices and, just in case you are still making up your mind, another section on 10 reasons the latest-generation Kindle is a must if you love to read. But this isn't rocket science: in fact, you'll find that the Kindle App comes already onboard with up-to-date devices like the Samsung Galaxy Tab, the Dell Streak, and many Windows 7 smartphones.)

So, the Kindle may have been rather expensive for early adopters back in 2007 and 2008, but it has become a very affordable staple for avid readers, including the Kindle Nation citizens we like to refer to as "the greatest readers in the world." And the chances are very good that, with the help of this book and the daily Free Book Alerts (http://bit.ly/h08fjy) on our Kindle Nation Daily blog (http://amzn.to/h4BmNz) , a new Kindle could actually save you hundreds of dollars over the course of a year or two.

For starters, did you know that the latest-generation Kindle 3G model (http://amzn.to/g2OXBL) also comes with a free built-in "Webkit" web browser and a free wireless "Whispernet" service that provides you with almost anywhere, anytime connectivity?

4

• Connectivity with Amazon and the Kindle Store, of course, so that you can keep buying Kindle books, magazines, newspapers, games and blogs, and be reading them on your Kindle within 60 seconds.

• Connectivity with Wikipedia, so you can look up anything that comes to mind or that you read about, within seconds.

• Connectivity with Amazon's Audible.com subsidiary, so that you can buy any of thousands of professionally-read audiobooks, download them wirelessly to your Kindle without a USB cable or computer, and start listening to them within moments.

But that's not all.

• You can also connect with Google, with your email, Facebook or Twitter accounts, or with just about any other text-based website!

• You can check scores, stocks, news, or weather, and then -- if you have a bit of patience and nimble fingers -- send an email, a text, or a tweet to share the news.

• You can read blogs, online documents, and news sources any time and any place you please.

Don't get me wrong: this is not a lightning-fast, full-featured browser. It's great in a pinch, but you aren't going to start using it to send dozens of email messages each day. But it *is* free, it is there when you need it, and it is quiet.

If, for instance, you are trying to read a real book on your Kindle, you will find the Kindle's connectivity is a lot less intrusive and distracting than most connected devices. It rests quietly in the background until you decide you need to use it for something.

And at that point, there's no need to find a Starbucks or other wi-fi connection.

There's never any need to pay a monthly wireless charge, a data fee, or an activation fee.

There's never a need to do anything but enjoy your Kindle.

Free.

But still, that's just the beginning.

Now that you've purchased this book, you are about to learn about millions of free books, games, blogs, articles, music tracks, podcasts, periodicals and research documents you can download to your Kindle in a snap, whether you are stocking up on beach reading or in the middle of a daunting research project.

Whatever you paid for your Kindle, the purpose of this ebook is to provide you with all the information, tips, tricks, and links you will need to make sure it begins paying for itself today and continues for each and every day you use it.

So, if you are still on the fence about whether to buy your first Kindle, or whether to upgrade from a Kindle 1 or Kindle 2, you may want to skip ahead for a few moments to Chapter 10, "Ten Reasons the Latest-Generation Kindle is a Must if You Love to Read."

Otherwise, let's get started.

Between the Chapters, and Just Between Us: Best Resources for Kindle Owners

This is a subjective list from someone with strong opinions. And, yes, I'm including a couple of my own free resources in this list. But the price is right on all of these, and you'll save money and time if you begin using them right now.

- Check out the Kindle Starter Kit (http://bit.ly/ig9eqM)at the Kindle Nation eBook Emporium for accessories and warranties.

- Make a daily appointment to check the free Kindle Nation Daily (http://bit.ly/fyFuTX) Free Book Alert each morning, or spend 99 cents a month for a Kindle edition subscription (http://amzn.to/h4BmNz) to have each post pushed directly to your Kindle.

- Check out the Internet Archive (http://www.archive.org/) for an incredible array of free content (details in Chapter 4).

- Follow podcaster Len Edgerly's The Kindle Chronicles (http://www.thekindlechronicles.com/) each Friday.

- If you are interested in reading Kindle content on an iPad, iPhone, or iPod Touch, see our sister blog Planet iPad (http://bit.ly/hdExVn).

- If you want to tap into some extremely intelligent deep thinking about the Kindle and other ebook readers, follow Abhi's Kindle Review (http://bit.ly/k-review).

Ch 2: Use Kindle Nation Daily's Free Book Alerts

Okay, you can call this a commercial if you want, because I'm touting my own Kindle Nation Daily blog (http://bit.ly/fyFuTX), but at least it's a commercial that will lead you to even more free books and content for your Kindle, such as the daily Free Book Alerts (http://bit.ly/h08fjy) published on the blog. If you don't want to bother checking the blog online each day, you can subscribe to Kindle Nation Daily and have each new post delivered direct to your Kindle automatically (http://amzn.to/h4BmNz).

Every morning we start things off at Kindle Nation with a Free Book Alert that is automatically updated to include the latest free contemporary titles in the U.S. Kindle Store.

You may have heard that many of the free books in the Kindle Store are classic public domain titles that are out of copyright and do not change from one week to the next. That's true, but there are also dozens of new contemporary freebies that are added each month. As of this writing in mid-December 2010, there are about 200 such free titles covering just about every reading taste and genre.

But these titles change from day to day: Amazon (and the authors and publishers who offer them free) giveth, and they also taketh away.

So, how do you make sure that you don't miss out on these free listings?

The answer is that we have your back at Kindle Nation, and all you have to do is make sure that you check in with us each morning, because there are many times when a free listing lasts only for a day or two, and some cases where it is gone within hours. To make sure you don't miss them, you can do one or both of these things:

• Bookmark Kindle Nation Daily (http://bit.ly/fyFuTX) on the web and make checking it part of your daily routine on the computer; and/or

• Even better, click here to subscribe to the Kindle edition of Kindle Nation Daily (http://amzn.to/h4BmNz) and each Free Book Alert post will be pushed directly to your Kindle 24/7 in real time. Your blog subscription begins with a free 14-day trial. After that, the full cost of this Kindle-compatible convenience is just 99 cents a month on your Amazon account, and it is likely to save you many times that amount as you build your personal Kindle library.

In addition to helping you keep up with what's free and what's worth reading in the Kindlesphere, our Kindle Nation Daily blog also mixes in other posts with useful tips and tricks for getting the most out of your Kindle, Kindle news, free excerpts, and a popular "From the Kindle Nation Mailbag" feature where you will find answers to questions that have been posed by your fellow Kindle owners, and possibly even by you. (We're always happy to hear from readers who email us at KindleNation@gmail.com.)

Thousands of Kindle Nation citizens also find it useful to receive a weekly digest of these posts in the form of a free weekly email newsletter. You can check out past newsletters, and sign up for future issues, at the Kindle Nation Archive (http://bit.ly/KindleNationArchive) site.

Between the Chapters, and Just Between Us: No Kindle Required! How to Download and Use Free Kindle Apps for the PC, Mac, iPad, iPhone, iPod Touch, BlackBerry, Android and, Soon, the Windows Phone 7 and Other Devices

The Kindle Store isn't just the best ebook store for the Kindle itself. It's also the best ebook Store for the iPad and all the other devices noted above. You can use one or more of these other devices to supplement reading on your Kindle, or -- just as easily -- you can make one of the other devices your primary ebook reader and get along just fine without a Kindle!

You can also start building a Kindle library now with one or more of these apps and decide later about whether you are ready to commit to a long-term relationship with a Kindle or some other gadget.

Just follow these steps to download the Kindle reading software and store interface to the device of your choice, absolutely free of charge:

• On your computer, sign into the Amazon.com account (http://amzn.to/dQzutW) that you use, or will use, for buying Kindle books.

• Visit the Kindle's main page for downloading free apps for other devices (http://amzn.to/dQMQcF) and select your device.

• Follow the prompt on the specific device app page to download the app directly or select it from the device-specific app store noted (such as the Android Market or the iTunes app store).

• Once you install the app on your device, you will be able to see all of the Kindle books that you own under "Archived Items" and move any of them directly to that device's Kindle Home screen.

Happy reading!

Ch 3: Find and Download Thousands of Free Books Directly From the Kindle Store

Have you heard that most books in the Kindle Store are priced at $9.99?

If so, it might seem like a lot to pay for a digital book, when neither the publisher nor the author incur any expense for printing, paper, shipping, returns, or warehousing. Ebooks at $10 a pop can add plenty to your monthly credit card bill in a hurry.

Well, here's some good news.

Over 39% of the books in the Kindle Store are priced at $4.99 or less, and among those there are -- as of December 2010 -- over 16,700 free books.

Another 46% are priced between $5 and $10, and of those that are priced above $10, the vast majority are technical books whose paper editions are far more expensive. That's right: about 85% of the books in the Kindle Store are under 10 bucks.

Each morning at Kindle Nation we publish a Free Book Alert (http://bit.ly/hO8fjy) focusing on the latest contemporary or promotional titles to be added to our Free Book listings (http://bit.ly/fdQVI3), and as I write this in December 2010, that list has grown to nearly 200 titles. It's one of the most popular things we do on the Kindle Nation blog, and it's a good feeling to know we are helping to keep Kindles everywhere, including our own, filled to the gills with good reading. (Watch for a future post that will help you locate your Kindle's gills).

You may also want to bookmark the Free Book Listings in Kindle Nation's eBook Emporium dedicated Amazon store -- at http://bit.ly/KNDeBookStore -- where you can find free book lists sorted to include or exclude certain categories, such as free erotica listings.

But the other 16,500 free books in the Kindle Store are nothing to sneeze at, either. While it is true that they are public domain titles, many of these are classics that make great leisure or enrichment reading. And if you happen to be an English, philosophy, or humanities major or graduate student, those classics could save you a bundle when it's time to buy textbooks. Not to put too fine a point on this, but these are not junk titles -- just type the name of one of your favorite classic authors into your search and you will likely be pleased with the return, especially when you see the prices.

Would you like an example? Well, here's a pretty good one, as of early December 2010. Just the other day, over 10 million Americans watched Oprah Winfrey hold up a copy of her latest Oprah's Book Club pick, a two-novel volume containing Charles Dickens' classics *Great Expectations* and *A Tale of Two Cities* (http://amzn.to/gAxDbJ). It was a bit of an interesting pick, since Oprah admitted on the air that she had never read anything by Dickens. But she held up a nice thick paperback that she said Penguin had published for her in just a week, with a suggested retail price of $20, discounted to $11 by Amazon. And she also held up a Kindle, in recognition of the fact that Amazon had provided her with a free Kindle for every member of her studio audience.

And yes, it is true that Penguin has also provided a Kindle edition of the two-novel Oprah's Book Club pick selection for the fairly reasonable price of $7.99 (http://amzn.to/flDXXa).

STEPHEN WINDWALKER

But the really good news for you and me and all of the hundreds of new Kindle owners in Oprah's audience is that -- with our Kindles -- those Dickens novels are absolutely free! We can click here for *Great Expectations* (http://amzn.to/hDqjDp) and click here for *A Tale of Two Cities* (http://amzn.to/et5NuX), and without spending a ha'penny we can start reading either or both books within seconds on any Kindle or Kindle app!

Now ain't that just the dickens? And maybe that's why the studio audience, after applauding politely for the Michael Jackson segment, the Jonathan Franzen rapprochement, and the Dickens picks, saved its most intense applause of Oprah's hour for the announcement that they had all received brand new, free Kindles!

Do you need a passcode or a secret handshake to access those free books? No, it couldn't be easier to find and download them wirelessly to your Kindle within seconds at no charge.

While it is generally true that you will be able to search the Kindle Store more effectively -- and more price-consciously -- from a computer or even a tablet than from your Kindle, it is certainly possible to get a listing of public domain titles in the Kindle Store while searching with your Kindle. Here are the basic steps:

•   From your Kindle, just go to the Kindle Store and type "Public Domain Books" (without the quotation marks) into the search field.

•   Your Kindle will soon display search results of over 16,500 titles.

•   If you want to narrow these results by category, just use your Kindle's 5-way controller or scroll-wheel to select "Narrow Results by Category" in the upper-right corner of the display screen.

•   Click on any title to check the price before buying, and select the "Buy" or "Try a Sample" button to download all or part of the book to your Kindle.

As is often the case with Kindle Store searches, you can see a lot more information and make a more informed choice about which books -- and which editions -- you want to buy or sample if, whenever possible, you do your searching from a computer or tablet. Here are a couple of helpful links that will help you find just the kind of free books that you are looking for in the Kindle Store:

• Go to http://bit.ly/FreeKindleStoreBooks for a listing of "over 16,700" free Kindle books of all kinds. Why did I put "over 16,700" in quotation marks? Well, it's because -- although there are 16,700 there -- Amazon limits your search to 120 pages, so you may think you have to surrender after viewing the first 4,800 free Kindle titles. *Do* you have to surrender? No, just click on one of the category links in the left sidebar to narrow your search within specific categories of free Kindle books.

• Still recovering from high school English, or just want to give the classics a rest for some other reason? Go to http://bit.ly/KindleFreebies for a listing that excludes all the public domain titles, so you'll only see those contemporary Kindle books whose authors or publishers have set the price at zero, generally as a promotion to stir up interest in a new title or the same author's more recent book.

• While we're at it, you can also get a heads up on Kindle titles -- of all prices -- that are so new they have yet to be released, just by going to this web address, just for fun: http://bit.ly/ForthcomingKindleTitlesNow .

Between the Chapters, and Just Between Us: Using Wi-Fi, 3G, or a USB Cable to Connect Your Kindle

Knowing the kind of connection that your Kindle (or Kindle app) uses to connect with Amazon, its proprietary "Whispernet," and the internet can save you money and time.

If you purchased a 6" Kindle anytime since July 2010, it is equipped with "wi-fi" connectivity that allows you to connect, free, using a local wi-fi network found in many homes, offices, coffee shops and other locations. Depending on the model, your Kindle may also have wireless 3G connectivity, similar to a cellular phone connection. 3G is great for downloading Kindle ebooks and even to access the web from just about anywhere, but if you have wi-fi connectivity and a wi-fi network, you'll want to use wi-fi because it's faster and cheaper for all concerned.

So let's keep it simple: if you have wi-fi, use the wi-fi whenever you can. Press the Menu button from the Home screen, select "Settings," and use the 5-way to select "view" next to Wi-Fi settings. Your Kindle will scan and display available Wi-Fi networks within its range. Choose yours, select "connect," and type in your Wi-Fi password if prompted to do so. You should only need to do this once in any location. (Go to http://amzn.to/fEnLc8 for more information on setting up your Kindle wi-fi).

If you got your 6-inch Kindle anytime before July 28, 2010, or if you own a Kindle DX, your Kindle probably depends solely on Amazon's 3G wireless "Whispernet" connection to connect with Amazon, the Kindle Store, or the internet. Although the connection itself is provided free of charge with no monthly fees, Amazon will apply some small charges for transfer of personal documents, including some (otherwise) free content from sources described in this book. (Go to http://amzn.to/f7hLuo for more information on Amazon's document transfer charges).

However, it is easy to avoid such charges in these ways:

• Use wi-fi if you have it.

• If you don't have wi-fi, use your USB cable to transfer content from your computer to your Kindle. (Go to http://amzn.to/fLZs3i for more information of transferring content with the USB cable).

Use your you@free.kindle.com rather than your you@kindle.com email address to convert and send documents to your computer for transfer to your Kindle.

Ch 4: Find and Download Free Books From Kindle-Compatible Free Book Collections

It used to be complicated, but now it's a snap.

When the Kindle first appeared on the scene late in 2007, many of us moved quickly to find ways to transfer free books from various digital content websites onto our Kindles for reading. Unfortunately, such transfer processes could get a little complicated at times, and invariably involved using one's computer and a USB cable as the "middle man" in the process.

Now, in a clear sign that the Kindle platform has arrived and is well on its way to maturity as an ebook reader, there are several very fine web-based Kindle-compatible services that streamline the process of finding and downloading free books so you can do this wirelessly, or via USB connection, or even directly from your Kindle, just about anywhere and anytime.

While some ebook retailers (such as the Barnes & Noble NookStore, Apple's iBookstore, and Google's eBookstore) have used titles from these non-profit services to inflate their catalog listing counts in an attempt to appear competitive with the Kindle store, Amazon keeps the vast majority of these titles separate and instead refers to them as Kindle-compatible "Free Book Collections." These web-based collections are composed primarily of about 2 million older, out-of-copyright, pre-1923 books and Amazon has worked with the services to enhance compatibility so that the books and other documents can be read directly with any Kindle or, also, with the Kindle apps for the PC, Mac, iPad, iPhone, iPod Touch, BlackBerry, or Android device. One reason for counting these titles "outside" the Kindle Store, of course, is that the majority of books included are created by scanning library or other copies of physical books, and their quality can vary widely.

For each of the services and procedures described below, it is your choice whether to download first to a computer using your Kindle for Mac or PC app, or -- where possible -- directly to your Kindle. Unless I know exactly what I am getting, my own preference is often to download a digital book to my computer using the Kindle for Mac app, because it is very fast and allows me to check a book for quality before placing it on my Kindle. Then, if I want to send it to my Kindle, I simply make sure that my Kindle 3's wi-fi connectivity is turned on, and email the file as an attachment to my [Kindle username]@free.kindle.com email address. The ebook then appears on my Home screen within seconds, without any charge.

This [Kindle username]@free.kindle.com email address feature only works for Kindles with wi-fi. If your Kindle is not equipped with wi-fi, you have a choice of transferring the file via your USB cable or paying a small fee (15 cents for the first megabyte and an additional 15 cents for each additional MB) to email it to the you@kindle.com email address that's available for *all* Kindle owners.

On the other hand, downloading directly to your Kindle can be so fast and convenient that I might be moved to call the process magical and revolutionary if Steve Jobs had not already trademarked those words. If you are taking this direct route, I recommend that you start with your Kindle's wireless switched "on" and that, once you go to the web, you use the Kindle Menu and Settings features to select "Enable Javascript" and "Article mode" or "Advanced mode" (or "Desktop Mode" if you are using the Kindle DX).

To reach the "Basic Web Settings" display screen, press the "Menu" button while you are in the Kindle web browser mode, and select "Settings" with the 5-way or scroll wheel. When you arrive at the Settings page, make sure that your Kindle is set to "Advanced Mode" on the top line of this screen -- or "Desktop Mode" if you are using the Kindle DX - - and to "Enable Javascript." If you do not anticipate using images as you make use of the Kindle 2 web browser, you can speed up its capacity to process content by selecting "Disable Images" on the bottom line of this display screen.

Project Gutenberg

The venerable, volunteer-operated, and donation-funded Project Gutenberg is the sine qua non of the public domain digital content movement with a vast and growing library of about 30,000 classics and more recently published books, and much of the content on the other services came originally from Project Gutenberg, so it will be my first focus here. Once you get the hang of downloading free classics from Project Gutenberg, the other services should come naturally.

In an earlier edition of this material we provided links to more than twice as many web-based free book websites, but we decided it does readers no favors to clutter the book with listings of websites in competition with the sites that we do list here, particularly since many of the competing sites do so by ripping off the original work of pre-existing sites. And frankly, if you can't find a public domain title on Project Gutenberg, the Internet Archive, or Open Library, it is highly unlikely you'll find it somewhere else.

Project Gutenberg was founded nearly 40 years ago by Michael Hart, and although we will be focusing on the PG Mobile site here, I encourage you to check out its main website (http://bit.ly/fRu12x) and its Wikipedia entry (http://bit.ly/hdmJje) to get an appreciation for an inspiring story of a real movement of people committed to a communitarian ideal that has gathered around the work and steadfast commitment of the founding individual. You will also find a PayPal "donate" button on the Project Gutenberg main page, and I hope you will do as I try to do and send them a buck now and then, even if it means separating the quarters from the lint in your change pocket.

The volunteers at Project Gutenberg have worked very hard to make the site better and better for Kindle users and everyone else who is interested in digital reading. With the new PG Mobile web presence, it is a snap to find a classic like Charles Dickens' *A Tale of Two Cities* or any of about 30,000 other titles and download them wirelessly to your Kindle.

For instance, to begin downloading *A Tale of Two Cities* wirelessly to your Kindle:

• Make sure your wireless is turned on and open your Kindle web browser.

• Next, visit the Project Gutenberg mobile site, called PG Mobile, at http://m.gutenberg.org/ , which is shown below.

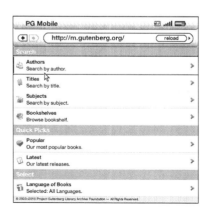

Once you've typed this URL into your Kindle's browser, you will probably want to add a bookmark for this main page for the PG Mobile site to your Kindle browser's bookmarks by pressing "Menu" and selecting "Bookmark This Page" once you are on the page.

•   Select Authors, which among the available choices is often the easiest way to begin a search if I know pretty much what I am looking for.

•   Select Charles Dickens from the Authors list.

•   Select A Tale of Two Cities from Dickens' titles.

•   When metadata for A Tale of Two Cities appears on your Kindle display, you will probably need to press your Kindle's "next page" button to see the download formats available.

•   Select the Kindle download format from among several formats offered (as shown on the following page).

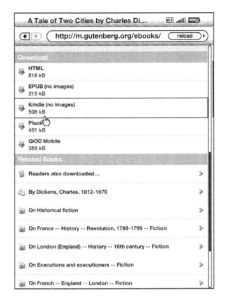

- Select "Yes" when prompted to download the file (shown on the following page).

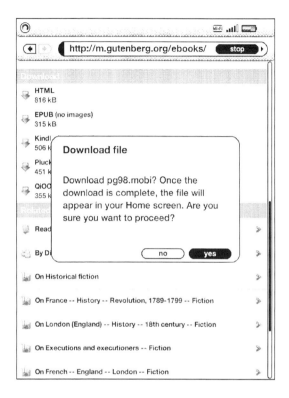

• When your Kindle display shows you that its web browser has successfully downloaded the file, press the Home button.

• Make sure that your Home screen is sorted "By Most Recent First" and, within a few seconds, you will find A Tale of Two Cities at the top of the screen.

• Open the ebook from your Kindle's home screen and enjoy.

I. The Period

It was the best of times,
it was the worst of times,
it was the age of wisdom,
it was the age of foolishness,
it was the epoch of belief,
it was the epoch of incredulity,
it was the season of Light,
it was the season of Darkness,
it was the spring of hope,
it was the winter of despair,

we had everything before us, we had nothing before us, we were all going direct to Heaven, we were all going direct the other way— in short, the period was so far like the present period, that some of its noisiest authorities insisted on its being received, for good or for evil, in the superlative degree of comparison only.

There were a king with a large jaw and a queen with a plain face, on the throne of England; there were a king with a large jaw and a queen

1%   Locations 37-44   6181

Naturally, as you've walked through this particular quest with me, you've noticed that there are plenty of other ways to search and browse for free Kindle-formatted books on the PG Mobile site, and thousands of good reasons for searching!

Internet Archive - Over 2.5 Million Free Titles

The Internet Archive is a non-profit organization dedicated to offering permanent access to historical collections that exist in digital format. In addition to various other forms of content, the Archive provides over 2.5 million free ebooks to read, download, and enjoy.

Although the Internet Archive does not presently have a site that is formatted for mobile access, it is possible to find books and download them wirelessly and directly to your Kindle by entering the URL http://archive.org/texts in your Kindle web browser. Search and browse the site with the browser, use the 5-way to select a title, and select the Kindle format. The download will begin immediately.

Unless your eyesight is very good and your fingers are very nimble, you are likely to find it more convenient to access the Internet Archive with your computer. Just go to the same Internet Archive texts page mentioned above (http://archive.org/texts) and search for a title, or browse one of the sub-collections, like American Libraries (http://amzn.to/hM8vBo).

When viewing a title, click the link on the left labeled "Kindle" to select the right format and download the file to your computer. Once you've downloaded an Internet Archive ebook or document to your computer, if you own a Kindle with wi-fi connectivity, just email the file as an attachment to your [Kindle username]@free.Kindle.com email address and Amazon will send it directly to your Kindle so that it appears on your Kindle Home screen in seconds.

If you have an earlier-generation Kindle without wi-fi, you can attach your Kindle to your computer using your USB cable and drag the file to the "Documents" folder on your Kindle. You can also e-mail the file wirelessly to your Kindle over a 3G connection, but be aware that Amazon will charge your account 15 cents for the first megabyte and an additional 15 cents for each additional megabyte.

Open Library - Over 1 Million Free Titles

Open Library's goal is to provide a page on the web for every book ever published. They've made a good start with over a million titles, and they have made downloading these titles to your Kindle easy as 1-2-3-4-5.

To get started, just visit the Open Library (http://openlibrary.org/) website in your computer's browser and make sure to check the 'Only show eBooks' checkbox near the top right-hand corner of the page.

You can use keywords to search for a title or browse by author, subject, list, or recent addition. Once you find a title to read on your Kindle, just click the 'Send to Kindle' link next to the edition in which you're interested. Open Library will then take you seamlessly to Amazon.com to enter your account information and select the Kindle to which you want to send the book. Delivery will be free to any Kindle with an active wi-fi connection; transfer charges will apply if a 3G connection is used.

Once you make a selection, you will be able to open the ebook from your Kindle's home screen and begin reading within a few seconds.

Other Free Book Websites

Compared with the fare and the easy processes described above, it may seem a bit labor-intensive to just troll the web looking for free books you can read on your Kindle. But it can also be rewarding.

While some of the websites we recommend below will require you to do some reformatting, saving, and transferring to your Kindle via a USB connection with your computer, others are more user-friendly. Two that are well worth checking out are the ManyBooks (http://manybooks.net) website, where you can explore a remarkable selection of free content that you can download to your Kindle, and the science fiction publisher Baen Books' Baen Free Library (http://bit.ly/f1LFNk).

These sites are wonderfully user-friendly -- just find a title by author, title, or the search field, select "Kindle" from the pull-down list of available formats, click on download, and the title will be on your computer drive within seconds. You can shoot it on to your Kindle email address (or transfer it via USB) in another 15 seconds or so.

Between the Chapters, and Just Between Us: Easily Find Free Kindle Store Classics Arranged by Author and Title

Before you go searching other websites for novels and stories by classic authors from Jane Austen to Jack London, you'll want to check the Kindle Store, and colleague Morris Rosenthal has made it delightfully easy to do this with a new web page that he has created at http://bit.ly/gO76MA. Here's a list of the authors featured as of December 2010:

Louisa May Alcott | Hans Christian Andersen | Elizabeth von Arnim | Jane Austen | Honoré de Balzac | L. Frank Baum | E. F. Benson | Marie Le Prince de Beaumont | M. E. Braddon | Charlotte Bronte | Frances Hodgson Burnett | Edgar Rice Burroughs | Lewis Carroll | Willa Cather | G. K. Chesterton | Agatha Christie | Wilkie Collins | Joesph Conrad | James Fenimore Cooper | Daniel Defoe | Charles Dickens | Fyodor Dostoyevsky | Sir Arthur Conan Doyle | Theodore Dreiser | Alexandre Dumas | George Eliot | Juliana Horatia Gatty Ewing | Edna Ferber | Henry Fielding | Dorothy Canfield Fisher | F. Scott Fitzgerald | Gustave Flaubert | E. M.

Forster | Mary Wilkins Freeman | R. Austin Freeman | Elizabeth Cleghorn Gaskell | Johann Wolfgang von Goethe | Zane Grey | Jacob and Wilhelm Grimm | H. Rider Haggard | Thomas Hardy | Nathaniel Hawthorne | O. Henry | Hermann Hesse | Mary Jane Holmes | Washington Irving | Henry James | James Joyce | Rudyard Kipling | Andrew Lang | D. H. Lawrence | Joseph Sheridan Le Fanu | Jack London | Hugh Lofting | W. Somerset Maugham | Herman Melville | George Meredith | A. A. Milne | John Milton | L.M. (Lucy Maud) Montgomery | Karen Niemann | Kathleen Thompson Norris | Marie Conway Oemler | Baroness Emmuska Orczy | Edgar Allan Poe | Beatrix Potter | Howard Pyle | Ayn Rand | Mary Roberts Rinehart | Marshall Saunders | Sir Walter Scott | George Bernard Shaw | Mary Shelley | Upton Sinclair | Robert Lewis Stevenson | Bram Stoker | Harriet Beecher Stowe | Gene Stratton-Porter | Jonathan Swift | William Makepeace Thackeray | Leo Tolstoy | Anthony Trollope | Ivan Sergeevich Turgenev | Mark Twain | Jules Verne | H.G. Wells | Elizabeth Wharton | Oscar Wilde | P. G. Wodehouse | Virginia Woolf | Johann David Wyss

Ch 5: Find and Download Free Book Samples and Free 14-Day Periodical Trials From the Kindle Store

While it is certainly true that a Kindle in the hands of an avid reader like you or me can quickly lead to some significant expenditures for reading materials, it is also true that Amazon has designed the Kindle, and arranged the Kindle Store, to make it easy for us to sample any Kindle edition before we buy it. Once you get the hang of using the free sample chapters for Kindle books, or the 14-day free trials for blogs and periodicals, you may find they provide you with a great way to look before you buy.

First, try out the Kindle's terrific *sampling* feature. Whether you are browsing titles directly from your Kindle or on your computer, the Kindle edition detail page for just about any title in the Kindle store will show a button on the right that allows you to send a sample chapter or two (usually between 5 and 10 per cent of the full text) directly, and pretty much instantly, to your Kindle. What's not to like about that?

STEPHEN WINDWALKER

The sample will download directly and wirelessly to your Kindle just as the complete book would, and the title will be displayed on your Home screen with the word "Sample" in a small font just to the left of the title line.

You can also download such samples to any device on which you have a free Kindle app, including a PC, Mac, Android device, BlackBerry, iPhone, iPod Touch, or iPad. Even if you do most of your reading on a Kindle, you may find that keeping a sample library on another device is a great way to reduce clutter on your Kindle home page and organize your decisions about books you might want to buy later.

Once you have a sample on your Kindle, it is easy to make a buying decision directly from your Kindle either by pressing the menu button and selecting "Buy this Book Now", or by going to the end of the sample, where you will find a link to buy the book.

One important warning: do not assume a book you have sampled will necessarily continue to be offered at the same price you noted when you first looked at it in the Kindle Store. For this and other reasons, I usually look at a book's Kindle Store product page *on my computer* before clicking to buy, rather than clicking to buy it from my Kindle or while reading the sample.

One other, relatively new way to sample Kindle books is with the Kindle for the Web feature that is still in the beta phase of its launch as we go to press. For all the latest information on Kindle for the Web, and samples of some great Kindle reads, check out our Kindle Nation Daily (http://bit.ly/fyFuTX) blog.

Perhaps because of confusion between the Kindle books free sample program and the free 14-day trials for periodicals and blogs, some Kindle owners have been concerned that book samples might automatically roll over and morph into purchases. For instance, on Amazon's discussion page for one of my books, Elizabeth from Fort Worth wrote in: "If you leave your sample on [your Kindle] too long, will they eventually charge you for it?"

Elizabeth, Amazon should never charge you for a sample of a Kindle book. If you feel you have been charged wrongly, it's worth a call to the Kindle Customer Support number at 1-866-321-8851 to seek redress. Be sure to have the identifying information for the charge in front of you when you call.

However, if you sign up for the "sample" form of a Kindle blog, newspaper, or magazine, which is a 14-day free trial, charges will begin immediately after 14 days unless you cancel the free trial by the end of the trial period.

Also keep in mind:

You can't easily cancel a Kindle periodical directly from your Kindle*. Instead, go to your Manage Your Kindle (http://amzn.to/hP7bma)page on Amazon.com from your computer. Scroll down to "Your active Kindle subscriptions" and you'll find it easy to cancel any subscription using the link to its right. (If you have a lot of Kindle subscriptions and you want to see them all at once without going through intermediate steps and extra clicks, use this link to see Manage Your Kindle Subscriptions in "View All" mode: http://amzn.to/fGlctH.

* If a 14-day free trial ends and Amazon begins charging you for the subscription, all is not lost. You can still cancel the subscription following the same process outlined in the paragraph above, and Amazon will refund -- at the least --

the pro-rated amount for the portion of the subscription month that you have not received yet.

As of December 2010, Amazon has announced it will soon make Kindle periodicals -- including their free 14-day trials -- available on Kindle apps for other devices, starting with the Android platform. This availability will be subject to publisher opt-out, and Amazon is already showing a "Tell the Publisher I'd like to read this publication on Kindle Reading Apps" link (http://amzn.to/eYzbWb) on the pages of periodicals whose publishers have yet to enable participation.

Between the Chapters, and Just Between Us: Free for You: How to Ask for and Use a Kindle Gift Certificate

Whether you are a student contemplating Kindle textbook purchases or just a happy Kindle owner of any age who is blessed with loved ones who want to feed your need to read, there's more than one path to "free" with the Kindle. If you have family or friends who want to help with your Kindle reading budget, the easiest way for them to help is to send you a Kindle Gift Certificate.

You or your loved ones can designate the design for a Kindle Gift Card (http://amzn.to/g4BCih) and set any amount from $5 to $5,000.

To ask for a Kindle gift card as a gift, just email the Kindle Gift Card link provided above to the person you're asking. Be sure, when it comes time to redeem the card amount, that you use the email account that is associated with your main Amazon account, the same account that you use for Kindle purchases.

To order a Kindle gift card, gift certificate, or email a gift credit in any quantity or any amount from $5 to $5,000, to anyone including yourself, just use the same link provided above, look for the "click to select design" link, and use the "Select" button to choose the "Amazon Kindle" gift card. Complete your purchase and you're all set.

(That's right, sending a Kindle gift card to yourself can be a good way to streamline your Kindle purchases or, perish the thought, stay on a budget!)

When you receive a gift card, go to http://amzn.to/eGJC11 to redeem the card and add the amount seamlessly to your balance. Available for Kindle or other Amazon purchases.

Ch 6: Use Calibre to Manage Your Kindle's Free Books and Other Kindle Content

Any Kindle owners interested in getting the most out of free content on the Kindle -- or paid content, for that matter -- should make a point of getting familiar with one of the greatest Kindle apps to come along yet, called Calibre.

Calibre provides features for a wide range of different ebook platforms and devices, but the fact that it supports the Kindle so elegantly is bound to make it a favorite with Kindle owners. In this chapter we will focus on Calibre's usefulness in managing, accessing, reading, and maintaining accurate metadata for the ebooks that you may have acquired based on the tips in Chapter 4.

According to its creator Kovid Goyal, Calibre was designed to make managing your ebook collection as easy as possible, and can be used to manage books, magazines, newspapers, comics and virtually any other kind of digital content. And, like most of the files that you will be managing with Calibre, the Calibre application itself is free.

The Calibre application will reside on your computer and will provide a great interface between your computer and your Kindle that will make it easy for you to do any of the following:

•   Convert ebooks and documents from other formats -- including CBZ, CBR, CBC, CHM. EPUB, FB2, HTML, LIT, LRF, MOBI, ODT, PDF, PRC, PDB, PML, RB, RTF, SNB, TCR and TXT -- either to MOBI format so that you can read them on your Kindle or to a wide variety of other formats so that you can read them on your computer or on another mobile device. These other formats include EPUB, FB2, OEB, LIT, LRF, MOBI, PDB, PDF, PML, RB, SNB, TCR and TXT. (The Kindle supports AZW, MOBI, PRC, AZW1, TPZ, TXT).

•   Read any supported ebook format directly from the Calibre e-book viewer on your computer.

•   Send ebooks to directly to your Kindle library via USB cable without any need to pay for Amazon's conversion process.

•   Make corrections or changes in the "metadata" -- such as titles, authors' and publishers' names, publication date, tags, ratings, and other data -- that are associated with each of the ebooks on your Kindle. Without getting too far afield from the basic subject at hand here -- free content -- you may find that this ability to edit metadata can be a powerful tool in sorting, organizing, and managing the content on your Kindle.

In order to begin using Calibre, you'll need to download the free app to your computer. You can download the Calibre software in formats that are compatible, respectively, with Windows, OS X for the Mac, or Linux at the Calibre website (http://bit.ly/hRDQ3r).

I recommend that even before you download Calibre, you begin by watching Kovid's 8-minute "Grand Tour" video presentation on Calibre at http://calibre-ebook.com/demo. There is also a further 14-minute video tutorial that includes "power tips" for using Calibre at http://bit.ly/gnjeuV. As much as it is my usual style to go through and break down instructional material step-by-step, the fact is that Kovid and his team are constantly updating Calibre. So I believe it will be more beneficial to you, now that I hope that I have whetted your appetite about what Calibre can do for you and walked you to the front door of the Calibre site, if I simply suggest that you watch Kovid's video and review the material on the site. It is also well worth an occasional visit to the Calibre help page (http://calibre-ebook.com/help) to check for more recent presentations.

Once you download and open Calibre, you will find a very hospitable Welcome Wizard that will prompt you to designate a directory where you will store and manage your Calibre Library off-Kindle so you can begin taking advantage of the app's powerful feature set. Naturally, you will find that you have the greatest range of ebook management options for those files that are not restricted by Digital Rights Management (DRM), a subject we will explore in a later chapter.

Between the Chapters, and Just Between Us: Email eBooks, Memoranda, Scripts, Manuscripts, Directions, Recipes, Legal Briefs and Other Personal Documents to Your Kindle

Everybody's doing it. What's that?

Using their Kindle to read every kind of personal and professional document that they'll ever have to read, that's what.

Your Kindle comes with its own email address, set by Amazon. You can find it on your Manage Your Kindle (http://amzn.to/hDJBRE) page and change it if you wish. It is up to you to designate the only email addresses that will be approved to send personal documents to your Kindle, starting with your own personal email address, of course. In the "Your Kindle approved e-mail list" section, enter the e-mail address and select "Add Address."

Actually, your Kindle has two email addresses:

- [Kindle username]@free.kindle.com, and

- [Kindle username]@kindle.com.

Use the "free" version of the address whenever possible to send documents to yourself. They will be delivered via your wi-fi connection or to your computer without any charges. If you have to use a 3G connection to send documents to your Kindle, Amazon will apply a small transfer charge.

The following files can be sent wirelessly to your Kindle using this transfer process: Microsoft Word (.DOC), HTML (.HTML, .HTM), RTF (.RTF), JPEG (.JPEG, .JPG), GIF (.GIF), PNG (.PNG), BMP (.BMP), and PDF (.PDF). If you are sending a PDF and you want Amazon to convert it to a Kindle-compatible format with flowable text (and the ability to use Kindle features like "text-to-speech" with it), type "convert" without the quotation marks in the subject field of your email.

Documents sent to your Kindle will show up in your Home screen using the name you have given the file, so you will probably want to pay attention to the file name before you send it. The document must be sent as an attachment, and content included in the body of the email will not be transmitted.

Ch 7: Read Blogs, Periodicals, and Other Web Content for Free on the Kindle

Amazon might prefer that you get all your Kindle blogs and periodicals for a price in the Kindle Store, and those Kindle editions are tough to match when it comes to elegant formatting and the convenience of having new issues and posts pushed wirelessly to your Kindle in real time. However, there are a number of increasingly user-friendly ways to enjoy newspapers, magazines, and blogs free of charge on a Kindle, and we'll break them down and show you how in this chapter and the next.

Here are the basic approaches:

• You can use your Kindle's web browser to read any of millions of blogs and online periodical editions directly from the web.

• You can use any of several RSS feed services such as Google Reader to read content summaries on your Kindle and then click through to content that interests you.

•   You can use Instapaper to flag, sort, and organize interesting articles as you surf the web and send them individually or in digest form to your Kindle.

•   You can set up Calibre to fetch the latest issues of newspapers, magazines and blogs and transfer them directly to your Kindle via an easy-to-use Calibre-to-Kindle USB connection.

All of these feature are better than ever on the latest generation Kindle 3G (http://bit.ly/h4DgEb) and Kindle Wi-Fi models (http://bit.ly/flyANZ) for the following reasons:

•   Both models come with wi-fi, which is must faster than 3G for any activities other than reading an ebook or listening to an audio file.

•   These latest generation Kindle 3G and Kindle Wi-Fi models both come with the Kindle's relatively new WebKit web browser based on the same platform that powers the Safari web browser. It's still a bit slow, but it is miles ahead of the previous Kindle web browser.

•   These latest generation Kindle 3G and Kindle Wi-Fi models feature the new eInk Pearl display that renders 50 percent better contrast than previous Kindle displays, which is especially important when viewing web content formatted for a larger color screen.

• These latest generation Kindle 3G and Kindle Wi-Fi models provide other features to enhance web page viewing and reading, including Article Mode (a Menu selection while viewing any web page on these Kindles) and several different "zoom" options using the "Aa" font key or the Menu.

Reading Directly on the Web With the Kindle Web Browser

Kindle owner preferences vary widely as to whether they enjoy reading online content directly with the Kindle's web browser. I find that it can be very convenient, in a pinch, to use my Kindle to check or read some material that is important to me on the web, especially if I am away from my computer or a more full-featured internet connection and the information is available on a stripped down "mobile" site. The price is always right and the connection is quiet and inconspicuous, so nobody else is likely to notice if I divert my attention now and then during a less than scintillating meeting to check my Kindle for the score of a game that is in progress, the latest news, any new emails I may have received, or a stock price.

The extent to which such browsing, checking, and reading suits one's purposes usually depends on several things:

• A website's balance between text and graphics, since graphic-intensive websites are generally very slow to load on a Kindle and difficult to view on the Kindle 1 or the Kindle 2.

• How much content is involved. Unless one is viewing the web in landscape view and desktop mode on a Kindle DX, many web pages do not automatically format very elegantly on a Kindle screen. I don't mind putting up with some sloppy formatting if I am reading a paragraph or two, but when I am reading a 2,000-word *New York Times* article I prefer the kind of user-friendly formatting that I am accustomed to either with the Kindle edition of the *Times* or with the Calibre fetch process. That said, periodical, blog, and website articles that are compatible with the latest-generation Kindles' "Article Mode" Menu selection usually look great on my Kindle.

• Whether real time updates are involved. For instance, using the mobile MLB.com site (http://bit.ly/hyM8qV) to check on my beloved Red Sox works very well on the Kindle, and I can even refresh to keep up with a running play-by-play.

• Whether the particular websites that you frequent provide a stripped-down, user-friendly presentation for mobile devices.

• One's general patience and tolerance for the relatively slow web page downloads and occasional freezes that one experiences with the Kindle.

But I heartily recommend that you give the Kindle's web browser a try so you can see if there are specific websites for which it works well in your daily life or, say, if you are vacationing for a week in a rustic, wi-fi-free cottage among the Outer Cape's dunes.

To help simplify the process, I recommend you reorganize your Kindle's web browser bookmarks as follows:

• Open the web browser. I find that the easiest way to do this is to type anything – like "web" -- into the Kindle and move the 5-way to the right to select "Google". The Kindle begins a Google search for whatever I typed in, but more importantly, the browser is open.

• Once you are in the browser, press the Menu button and select "Bookmarks".

• When your list of web bookmarks appears on the Kindle display, note the bookmarks you will probably never use and delete them. For me, for instance, that meant deleting the bookmarks for Google and Wikipedia because it is far easier to open Google and Wikipedia from within the Kindle's onboard search (as described in the example two paragraphs above), and deleting some other bookmarks such as those for E! Online and a recipe website because, well, barring unforeseen changes in my personal DNA, I just know that I will never use them.

• Deleting a bookmark with the Kindle is an easy process. Just move the 5-way to that bookmark's line in the bookmark list, but instead of pressing down to select and open the bookmark, move the 5-way to the left to begin the deletion process and follow the on-screen dialog box -- it's the same process used for deleting items or samples from your Home screen.

• By deleting bookmarks that you will not use, you create space on the first page of your Kindle web bookmarks display to add, judiciously, the bookmarks you are most likely to frequent. Take some care with this process, because (to the best of my knowledge) you will not be able to change the order of appearance for whatever bookmarks populate your list: the list will always display with the bookmarks that you have kept from the original list in their original order, followed by the bookmarks that you add in the order that you add them.

• In order to add a bookmark, you must first go to the web page you want to bookmark, either by typing in the URL, finding it through a Google or other search, or using your 5-way or scrollwheel to click on a link in something you are reading on your Kindle.

• Once you are viewing a web page on your Kindle, you can easily add a bookmark for the page just by pressing the Menu button and selecting "Bookmark this page". (Note: If you seek to bookmark more than one page from a particular domain – as I have occasionally done with Google Mobile features -- you may occasionally run into a conflict when multiple bookmarks are read by your Kindle as having the same metadata title. I know of no solution for this problem other than to select my one best choice from these pages as the one which I will bookmark).

Setting Up a Google Reader RSS Feed for Your Kindle

What is Google Reader?

Google Reader is yet another nifty web-based service from Google. It aggregates content through RSS feeds from the web, based on each individual's tastes and selections and serves the content in real time to an individual's personal Google Reader page for reading on- or off-line. It is compatible through web browser platforms with a wide variety of devices, including the Kindle. For a delightfully simple, elegant, and useful 3-minute video about Google Reader in plain English, see this CommonCraft video: http://bit.ly/eyugxZ.

Using Google Reader To Read Your Favorite Blogs on the Kindle

For many Kindle owners, the Kindle is all about convenience, and there is nothing at all wrong with that. When it comes to reading blogs on the Kindle, you may be perfectly content to pay a monthly fee for the convenience of having blog posts organized and pushed directly to your Kindle for a great reading experience without a lot of accompanying clutter. You may even be satisfied with Amazon's selection of (at this writing) 10,876 blogs from which you may choose. If you're satisfied, you need not read further.

But there is another way.

By following the few, very easy steps outlined in this chapter, you can adapt Google Reader to your Kindle so that it fetches the blog content you are most interested in reading and pushes that content right to your Kindle's web browser where you may read it anywhere, anytime, and at absolutely no cost.

Set Up Your Google Accounts

The first step, if you haven't already taken care of this, is to establish a Google account. As you follow various suggestions from our Kindle Nation Daily blog (http://bit.ly/fyFuTX) for making the most of your Kindle, it is very likely that you will be using several features of your Google account including Google Reader, Gmail, Google

Blog Search, Google Search, Google Notebook, Google Calendar, Blogger, and Google News. Although we are still early in the Age of the Kindle, it is becoming increasingly clear that, whether or not Google and Amazon ever enter into any explicit joint agreements regarding services that optimize the Kindle, Google will be a steady source for useful enhancements for Kindle owners.

All of Google's services can be accessed through a single Google user account. For most people, the most convenient approach will be to use the same Google account with your Kindle that you use on your desktop or notebook computer. However, there may be some circumstances in which it is useful to employ separate accounts for different devices. For instance, if you use Google Reader to follow multimedia-intensive blogs on your computer, you may want to use a separate account for subscriptions to the more text-intensive blogs that are suitable for Kindle reading.

Bookmark Your Google Mobile And Google Reader Pages

Creating bookmarks for Google Reader and other mobile Google services in your Kindle's web browser will save you and your thumbs a lot of extra work in the future, and it is an easy process.

1. Make sure the Kindle's Whispernet wireless feature is on.

2. From your Kindle's "Home" screen, press the "Menu" button on the right edge of the Kindle.

3. Use the 5-way or scrollwheel to select "Experimental" from the menu selections, and then choose "Basic Web" from the "Experimental" page.

4. Once you are in the web browser, press the "Menu" button again and use the 5-way or scrollwheel to click on "Settings" from the menu selection. On the web browser's Settings page, enable (or verify that you have already enabled) Javascript and "Advanced" Mode (rather than "Default" Mode). Note: the web browser's Settings page is different from the Settings page accessible directly from your Kindle's "Home" screen.

5. Click on "Enter URL" at the top of the next screen and type the following into the input field to the right of the "http://" prefix:

m.google.com

6. When the Google Mobile products page loads onto your Kindle screen, move the 5-way or scrollwheel up or down to enter cursor mode and push down twice quickly on the 5-way or scrollwheel to bookmark the Google Mobile products page.

7. From the Google Mobile products page, use the 5-way or scrollwheel to select "Reader" from the Google Mobile products choices.

8. When the Google Reader page loads onto your Kindle screen, move the 5-way or scrollwheel up or down to enter cursor mode and push down twice quickly on the 5-way or scrollwheel to bookmark the Google Reader page.

You will then have bookmarks for the top-level Google Mobile products page and for the Google Reader page. You may, of course, follow similar steps to bookmark other Google pages that you expect to use.

How to Subscribe to Your Favorite Blogs With Google Reader

Generally speaking, you will find it much easier to use your computer, rather than your Kindle, to search out your favorite blogs and add them to your Google Reader subscriptions so you can then have easier access to them on your Kindle. It is an easy process:

1. Find a blog that you want to add to your Google Reader subscriptions. Find the RSS Feed button on the blog and copy the link for it. In many cases, you can simply type the blog's URL into the input field rather than looking for an RSS Feed button.

2. Open the main Google Reader page. The shortest URL I have found for this is reader.google.com. If you haven't already signed in with your Google account, do so.

3. From the "sidebar" column to the left of your Google Reader screen, select the Add Subscriptions link.

4. Copy the RSS feed link of the blog to which you want to subscribe into the input field that opens when you select the Add Subscriptions link. The blog will now be included in your Google Reader subscriptions. (As noted above, in many

cases, you can simply type the blog's URL into the input field rather than looking for an RSS Feed button).

How to Read Blogs on the Kindle With Google Reader

Once you have attended to the steps above, reading blogs on the Kindle is remarkably simple and user-friendly.

1. Make sure that your Kindle's Whispernet wireless feature is turned on.

2. From your Kindle's "Home" screen, press the "Menu" button on the right edge of the Kindle.

3. Use the 5-way or scrollwheel to select "Experimental" from the menu selections, and then choose "Basic Web" from the "Experimental" page.

4. Choose "Google Reader" from your Kindle web browser's bookmarks (the bookmark is there because you followed the steps in an earlier section to create it). The Bookmarks page is the "default" page that usually appears first when you enter the web browser, but if another page comes up instead, just push the "Menu" button (within the web browser) and use the 5-way or scrollwheel to select "Bookmarks."

5. When the "Google Reader" page loads to your Kindle screen, you may be required to provide the log-in name and password of your Google account, but generally you will only be required to do this when your browser's cache has been cleared either manually or by a system re-set. Once you log in, you are ready to start reading.

6. In order to "sort" your blogs and read only the posts on a particular blog, just click on "Subscriptions" from the "Google Reader" page and select the blog you wish to read. Generally, this will create a more pleasurable reading experience than jumping from one subject matter to another. It will also come in handy as a way of protecting you from losing track of the content on a two-posts-per-day blog that might otherwise be overwhelmed by posts from other blogs if you have subscribed to news site blogs or other prolific posters.

Surf and Send Interesting Web Content with Instapaper

Here's a cool web-based service that is primarily designed for Kindle owners. It makes it stunningly easy and convenient to grab interesting content on the fly from any website and read it later on your Kindle.

Just go to Instapaper.com, sign up for a free account, and link your account to your Kindle via your:

- [Kindle username]@kindle.com or

- [Kindle username]@free.kindle.com

email address. Grab the "Read Here" button, drag it and stick it on your browser's toolbar and you are ready to go. Wherever you surf on the web all day long, you can click that "Read Here" link and content that you select will be sent to your Kindle, in a reader-friendly digest file that will be easy to identify on your Home screen, whenever you want: on demand, once a day, or once a week.

Please note: Amazon will charge you 15 cents per Instapaper transmission and conversion to your Kindle via your [Kindle username]@kindle.com email address, as well as an additional 15 cents for each megabyte of the file's size beyond the first megabyte of any file. But if you have a latest-generation Kindle with wi-fi, just use your free [Kindle username]@free.kindle.com email address and there will be no charges.

Fetch the News, Newspapers and Magazines, And Other Content with Calibre

In Chapter 6 you learned how to use Calibre to manage your ebook library. Now we'll focus on how you can send Calibre out onto the internet to fetch entire periodicals on a regular basis online and, then, to deliver them in elegantly formatted files directly to your Kindle.

Once you have Calibre open on your computer, it's a snap to fetch free content from a growing list of great online sources. To get started, just click on the "Fetch news" icon near the top of the Calibre display and select "Schedule news download" from its pulldown menu:

STEPHEN WINDWALKER

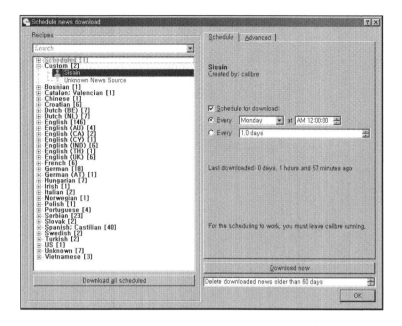

The next display to appear on your screen will allow you to select the language in which you wish to find online content. If you click on "English," you will see a list of content choices such as the one above. Just click on the periodical of your choice and Calibre will display dialog boxes to prompt you through the process of setting your preferences for scheduling regular downloading its content, with choices allowing you to complete your downloads at a time of your choice daily or on a certain day or days each week. The choice of the download time can be important for several reasons:

• You may want to make sure that a daily newspaper downloads at an optimal time to catch its most recent edition, such as 5 a.m.

• Calibre will complete your scheduled "Fetch news" downloads only if it is open on your computer.

• Calibre will push your scheduled "Fetch news" downloads automatically to your Kindle only if the Kindle is connected to your computer via USB cable.

Try it. I think you will like it, and you may be amazed at how nicely and fully Calibre renders your "Fetch News" content on your Kindle. For instance, the weekly fetch of the *New Yorker* comes complete with the new issue's cartoons, Goings on About Town listings, and helpful article summaries.

Between the Chapters, and Just Between Us: Use eReadUps to Collect Research on Your Kindle or Build Your Own eBooks from Web Sources

Working on a research or other information-gathering project and want to collect it in easy-to-read customized Kindle books of your own?

There's a great free tool waiting for Kindle owners at eReadUps (http://www.ereadups.com):

• Just choose the topic you want to read, type it into the box on the eReadUps website and click "Find Articles."

• eReadUps will search for related articles on the web and give you a list to select from.

• Choose the articles you want to include and build your own eReadUp "ebook" that you can read on your Kindle or another device.

Should research really be this easy?

Ch 8: Why Your Kindle's Free Wireless Web Browser is a Revolutionary Feature, and May Be the Key to What's Next from Amazon

When Amazon launched the Kindle in November 2007, and for the first 33 months of its existence, the service that Amazon calls Whispernet was a 3G EV-DO wireless broadband service that enables the Kindle to connect to Sprint's or AT&T's United States wireless data network. With the launch of the Kindle 3G+Wi-Fi and Kindle Wi-Fi models in August 2010, Amazon added the capacity for Kindle owners to use existing faster (and cheaper, to Amazon, at least) wi-fi networks in their homes, offices, coffee shops, libraries, or other locations.

But the 3G service remains one of the most distinctive things about the Kindle over three years after the initial launch, and cinches the four-pronged Kindle advantage of catalog, customer base, convenience, and connectivity over all other competitors in the ebook space. Other ebook reader manufacturers have taken tentative steps in the direction of wireless connectivity for their devices but in every case have closed off their systems in some fundamental way, either by blocking true web connectivity or by arranging for high prices for the data connection which is free for the Kindle.

The service is available in most densely populated areas in the United States, and throughout much of the rest of the world as well, but not everywhere. If your Kindle is within the carrier's United States wireless data network, you won't need a wi-fi connection, a computer connection, or any synchronization steps. The process of ordering a book from the Kindle store and then seeing it on your Kindle display is only slightly slower than the speed of thought. And now, with the addition of wi-fi connectivity, an even faster experience is available both within and outside the 3G coverage area.

When the original Kindle was launched in November 2007, the device's Whispernet-enabled "Basic Web" feature was designated as "experimental," which meant that it could be discontinued by Amazon at any time. There was considerable speculation on Kindle owners' message boards and elsewhere that the web connectivity would eventually be considered too expensive by Amazon and discontinued.

However, the service is a popular feature with many Kindle owners, whether one considers it ancillary or essential to the device's connectivity with the Kindle Store, which is the key commercial portal, of course, through which the Kindle connects our wallets and credit cards to Amazon's corporate bank accounts. And from our point of view as readers and book buyers, it is the portal through which Amazon is able to dazzle us with nearly instantaneous delivery of the books and other content that we want to read on our Kindles.

Although the Kindle has been marketed initially as an "e-book reader", its array of features actually sets the bar considerably higher than any of its predecessor e-book devices. Electronic reading devices have been around for decades, but until the launch of the Kindle they failed to gain any serious traction.

These ancillary Kindle features include audio, graphic, and even game-playing capacities, but foremost among them is the Kindle's free broadband wireless connectivity, which has significant benefits for the device's functionality both with e-books and with other content. Such a data connection ordinarily costs over $50 to $75 per month, but Amazon pays the entire bill (whatever it is), handles any problems with carriers, and uses the connection to run a "Whispernet" service that allows Kindle owners to download content -- books, newspapers, magazines, and blogs -- within seconds of purchasing it from the Kindle store.

One of the more intriguing aspects of the Kindle's initial rollout in November 2007 was the degree to which Jeff Bezos and Amazon played this most revolutionary feature so close to the vest. By marketing the Kindle as an e-book reader, Amazon kept the public focus away from the Kindle's stunning EV-DO wireless connectivity.

Why stunning?

Five main reasons:

• It allows seamless, simple, same-minute delivery of any content purchased in the Kindle Store.

• It transforms the Kindle into a web-browsing computer -- albeit a relatively slow one -- that can access nearly any website.

- It is fast -- essentially broadband over a cellular network -- although the speed of the connection itself is unfortunately brought low by the Kindle's slow processing speed.

- It is free, as compared with the $40 to $90 per month that you would pay to connect an iPhone, Blackberry, iPad or any other device to EV-DO or other wireless data services.

- The service is ubiquitous in well-populated areas, so that you never have to search for a wi-fi hot spot.

So, did you get this? Did I just tell you that you could buy a mobile computer for $189 with all of the above features, and never pay a dime to connect to the web?

That's right.

Now that Amazon has released a remarkably full-featured Kindle Wi-fi (http://amzn.to/gTeNS2) model for just $139, the $50 price differential between that model and the $189 Kindle 3G places an elegant value-proposition accent on the Kindle's wireless connectivity. If you think that either of these Kindles is worth $139 as an ereader, that just leaves this question:

Would you pay $50 one time, with no monthly fees or AT+T contracts, for wireless connectivity that would allow you to check email, scores, stocks, weather and any text-intensive website from just about anywhere for the rest of your life?

Well, I thought so.

Importantly, from the perspective of those of us who might occasionally want to use the Kindle's web browser, the new Kindle 3G model comes with:

• a *faster, more navigation-friendly, vastly improved but still absolutely free web browser* based on WebKit, the open-source Web browser engine that is also the basis for ... wait for it ... Apple's Safari web browser;

• a new *Article Mode feature within the updated web browser* that, similar to Instapaper, simplifies many articles and web posts to text-based content reading;

• an *automatic toggle between 3G wireless and wi-fi connectivity* that makes use of the best, fastest network available once you've synched it up with your home, office, or local coffee shop's wi-fi interface;

The first two of these features, of course, also come on the Kindle Wi-Fi.

The wireless service obviously has significant value. If Amazon made the service a user option with a service charge of, say, $12.95 a month, some users would pay the fee for the opportunity to use the web from nearly anywhere with such a portable, lightweight, easy-to-read device. Many others would opt out to the fallback of using their Kindle strictly for reading and visiting the Kindle Store -- sort of like using a Maserati as a student-driver car.

Will Amazon ever cut back on the Kindle's connectivity or begin charging for it? No.

Indeed, it is far more likely that Amazon will continue to build new lanes to expand the Kindle's internet highway into a much more profitable thoroughfare by introducing an entirely new model as early as February or March of 2011. It may be so new that it is not even called a Kindle -- Bufo Calvin, a very smart colleague of mine at the I Love My Kindle blog (http://amzn.to/eS8dhc), has suggested that a new Kindle-enabled tablet-like device might be called the

Amazon Current, and I think that would be a brilliant name for it for about half a dozen reasons.

Such a device -- with wireless connectivity and a color capacitative touch display, of course -- could act, once purchased, as Kindle-enabled delivery system not only for ebooks but for a growing list of other digital products sold by Amazon including audiobooks, music files, streaming movies and television, and a wide range of traditional and enhanced periodicals.

Stay tuned. As is so often true with Amazon, it will be interesting to see what's next.

Between the Chapters, and Just Between Us: Use Your Kindle to Check Your eMail

Don't try this at home. No, it's not that it is dangerous. It's just that it's a little slow and clunky.

But if you are off somewhere with a computer or another internet connection and you need to see if you have received an important email, your Kindle will do just fine.

Some users have had success using mobile-optimized sites for email with their Kindle, but in my experience you will do best if you set up your email via the email provider's main website, and I also recommend using Gmail if at all possible.

If you have a Gmail address, here's a simple set of steps for accessing your Gmail account for the first time on your Kindle.

• Open the Kindle web browser by Googling google. That's right: from anywhere on the Kindle, type the word "google" and when it appears in the entry field at the bottom of your display, press the 5-way to the right 3 times to initiate a Google search for Google.

• When the Google page appears on your screen, you will see a horizontally arranged list of Google services, including Gmail, at the top of the display. Use the 5-way to click on Gmail.

• When the Gmail page appears on your screen, type in your Gmail address and your password in the appropriate fields, check the "Stay signed in" box, and click on "Sign in."

• Your Gmail inbox should slowly populate the display, and you will be able to select and read messages. It is also possible to send a message, but only if you are very succinct and very patient.

• While you are on the Inbox page, use the Menu to add a bookmark for the page.

For other email services, there are no guarantees, but follow a similar process and there's a good chance you will be able to open your email.

Please note that the reason I suggested that you Google "google" rather than "gmail" is that Googling "gmail" is likely to bring you to a mobile Gmail site on which, based on my experience, you probably won't be able to enter text or your password.

Ch 9: Unlock the World Of Free Audio on the Kindle

On the Kindle, "Free" doesn't apply only to **_visual text_**.

Your Kindle also makes it easy to listen to several different kinds of content in audio form, and much of this, like almost everything we have discussed in this book, is free. Every Kindle comes with a built-in MP3 player and works seamlessly as a listening device for various kinds of listening files. The stereo speakers mounted on the back of the current generation of Kindles may not impress you, but they are stronger and richer and generally a big improvement over the tinny, barely audible external sound that emitted from the Kindle 1. To go one step better, you can use the audio-jack near the power switch on the top or bottom edge of your Kindle to connect it to a speaker system or headphones. On the bottom edge of the Kindle 3G and Wi-Fi, or the right edge of earlier models, you will find "down" and "up" volume-control buttons. I would go so far as to say that headphones or some other sort of external speaker are a must if you are using a first-generation Kindle, also known as a Kindle 1.

You'll find it easy to transfer MP3 versions of your favorite music, podcasts, and radio shows and listen to them free on your Kindle, and of course you will also find many of the free books and other files that you download from the Kindle Store or from other sources suggested in this book will work nicely with the text-to-speech feature on the Kindle 2, Kindle 3G, Kindle Wi-Fi or Kindle DX.

Before we begin discussing various kinds of free listening that is available on your Kindle, it is important underline two important caveats about the Kindle as an audio device:

•   First, audio files take up far more storage space on the Kindle or any other device than text-intensive ebook files, and you could very easily run out of Kindle storage space with multiple audio files unless you manage your space judiciously.

•   Second, using the Kindle's audio is, in my experience, the fastest single way to draw down the Kindle's battery charge. If you are going to listen to text-to-speech or any other audio feature on a Kindle for several hours at a time, be sure to have your power adapter and cable nearby.

Kindle Text-to-Speech

How do I love thee, Kindle Text-to-Speech? Let me count the ways. I have named thee, with a little help from an eyebrow-raising Significant Other who may a time or two have looked askance as I rolled over and donned my headphones of an evening. I have named my Kindle's voice Ursula. This imagined creature may or may not be disembodied, but she never seems to tire of reading to me, talking to me, entertaining me. When it's just me, my headphones, and Ursula, of course, it's all about me.

I will admit it: I love listening to newspaper, magazine, and blog articles, including my daily Instapaper dispatch, in the robot-speak of Ursula's Kindle Text-to-Speech. Originally I was resistant to listening to **books** with Kindle Text-to-Speech, but Ursula aims to please. Her voices and pronunciations have been upgraded over time by Kindle's Text-to-Speech partner, Nuance Communications, and I have grown accustomed to listening with comfort, enjoyment, and enrichment as she reads me free and paid books purchased in the Kindle Store, downloaded from the websites mentioned in this book, or sent to me by authors and publishers interested in having their work considered for Kindle Nation Daily sponsorships programs.

With the exception of those Kindle Store books whose publishers have specifically opted out of Kindle Text-to-Speech -- and shame on them! -- Kindle Text-to-Speech will read aloud to you from any book, newspaper, magazine, blog, manuscript, dramatic script, memorandum or other file that you can get onto your Kindle Home screen.

I've even sent recipes to my Kindle so that Ursula could read aloud to me while I was preparing Potage Parmentier in the kitchen.

And please don't tell the Massachusetts state troopers, but I have even sent driving directions to my Kindle so that it could read them aloud to me in my car. I've gotten handy at using the space bar to pause the read-aloud process, but I run into problems if a segment of my trip is longer than 15 minutes, because Ursula does have a tendency to doze off beside me if she goes that long without speaking. Alas, now that we've heard the horror stories of Kindle owners being arrested for having an open Kindle in the car while driving, I must ask you to destroy this page of the Kindle edition of your book immediately after you read it. A Kindle, apparently, is every bit as dangerous to highway safety as an open bottle of beer.

But that's just the beginning. Don't tell Ursula, but there's more, much more. It would be easy to overlook the device's other audio features, but they are still significant and they can add to your enjoyment of any member of the Kindle family.

Free Audiobooks

Amazon's own Audible.com audiobook subsidiary is wonderfully convenient to use, but some may find it a bit expensive.

A nice alternative that offers very polished voice actors' readings of thousands of classics from Shakespeare to *Ulysses* -- and every one of them *free* -- is the non-profit Librivox (http://librivox.org/) effort, a sister service of Project Gutenberg. The same content found there is also accessible through the Internet Archive, along with thousands of other additional free audio files, and in my experience the Internet Archive is slightly more user-friendly when it comes to finding files in the right MP3 format and downloading them first to your computer and then to your Kindle.

That, of course, is how you'll want to proceed, because audio files are generally too large to send to your Kindle via email, even using a wi-fi connection. To begin, go to http://bit.ly/f62Hhh to visit the Internet Archive's main audio page (over half a million free files) or to http://bit.ly/e9Yl5N for about 6,000 book and poetry files. Then you can just follow the on-site instructions to search for a title that interests you and download it to your computer's hard drive. Once an audio file is on your hard drive, connect your Kindle to your computer via USB cable and drag and drop the file from your computer into your Kindle's "audible" folder.

Always pay attention to your Kindle's storage capacity and remaining storage space, as audio files require much more storage space than text files. You can always check the remaining space available on your Kindle by pressing the "Menu" button and reading the "xxxx MB free" line to the left of the time on the top line of the display.

When an MP3 audio file is placed in your Kindle's "Audible" folder, it will appear on your Home screen with the word "Audible" next to the title in the left margin, and you will have the convenience of being able to use the same play, pause, and other commands that are present for Audible.com audiobooks. The same applies to music MP3 files that you place in the "Audible" folder, but another option with music -- or for that matter any other MP3 files -- is to place them in your Kindle's "Music" folder so they will be available for background listening while you read on your Kindle display.

How To Use The Kindle's "Play MP3" Feature To Play Background Music As You Read

For uses other than the "Read-to-Me" feature and listening to Audible.com files, the Kindle nomenclature for its audio functionality is "Play MP3," and it will work only with podcasts, music, or other audio files that are in an MP3 format and are not DRM-protected. (Although Kindle users often think of DRM or Digital Rights Management as an ebook issue, much of the world learned of DRM first in connection with music. For a good explanation of what is involved with DRM and music, see this article at Wikipedia: http://bit.ly/MusicDRM-Explainer.

In order to get listening material onto your Kindle you must transfer it from your computer, using the Kindle's USB cable, into your Kindle's native "music" file. Just find the file (or files) on your computer using the computer's "Finder" or "My Computer" application, copy it, and paste it into your Kindle's "Music" folder. Such files will often be found in your "My Music" folder, in a downloads folder, or on your computer's desktop. As mentioned earlier, pay attention to your Kindle's storage capacity and remaining storage space, as audio files require much more storage space than text files. As mentioned above, remember, you can always check the remaining space available on your Kindle by pressing the "Menu" button and reading the "xxxx MB free" line to the left of the time on the top line of the display.

Once you have listening files in the "Music" folder on board your Kindle, you may begin or end the use of the Kindle's audio feature by following holding down the "ALT" key on your Kindle keyboard and pressing the spacebar.

While listening to your Kindle's music or podcast files in Play MP3 mode, you'll generally be operating blind, since the Kindle plays whatever in its listening queue either in shuffle or sequential order (based on the order you transferred the files to your Kindle) without any on-screen reference. However, you can press the ALT+F key at anytime to skip to the next track, and pause or resume play by pressing ALT+Spacebar. The Kindle's MP3 player will continue to play if it is playing when you put your Kindle to sleep, but you will not be able to use these keyboard commands with the MP3 player unless you awaken your Kindle again.

I find the best way to manage the music I want to hear on my Kindle is to create several "playlist" folders in the top-level Kindle directory, each representing an appropriate selection for a particular situation. I might listen to jazz while reading a book, or something a bit more lyric-intensive while reading the New York Times. By moving a certain playlist into the Kindle's "Music" folder -- the only folder from which the Kindle will recognize and play music -- I can suit my listening to my situation in a couple of key strokes while the Kindle is connected to my computer. However, it is worth mentioning again that sound files can take up a large percentage of the Kindle's memory, and it may be more prudent to keep some of these files off-Kindle in a Kindle-management folder accessible through your computer's "Finder" or "My Computer" functions.

It is also a simple matter, retracing these same steps, to listen to podcasts on my Kindle once I move them from my computer to the Kindle's "Music" folder.

Podcasts and Other Uses of the Kindle's Audible Folder

How To Use The Kindle's "Audible" Folder And Features To Exercise Greater Control While Listening To Any MP3 Audio File -- Not Just Those You Download From Audible.com!

Although it is a pretty well-kept secret, you can also use the Kindle's "Audible" folder to play any audio file as long as you aren't going to be reading or making use of other features on your Kindle while you are listening. Two great things about this particular mode of listening are:

• the file will be listed on your Home screen (with the word "audio" to the left of the title); and

• you can use the same full set of features to navigate or replay the audio files that are available to you while listening to an Audible.com file, or for that matter, an iTunes file.

This "Audible" listening mode can be especially useful for a handful of favorite songs, or for listening to a podcast, such as Len Edgerly's weekly The Kindle Chronicles (http://bit.ly/KindleChronicles), on your Kindle. The ability to use the Kindle 5-way to go back or forward 30 seconds in a podcast makes this mode a pleasure to use.

Whether you follow your favorite podcasts directly from the web (as with the link to The Kindle Chronicles) or download them through iTunes, it's easy to transfer them to your Kindle's "Audible" folder. For instance, because I have subscribed to Ira Glass' *This American Life* podcast on iTunes, iTunes automatically downloads an MP3 file of each week's show to a folder (Music>iTunes>iTunes Music>Downloads>Podcasts>This American Life) on my iMac. Then I just go to that folder, copy the most recent file, paste it my Kindle's "Audible" folder, and I'm good to go. I can do the same with any other DRM-free MP3 audio file that resides on my computer's hard drive, including, for instance, tracks that I have downloaded to my iTunes folders from CDs that I have purchased and music files -- like the Mozart tracks mentioned in the next section -- that I have purchased from Amazon's MP3 Downloads Store (http://bit.ly/MP3s-For-Kindle).

All you have to do to opt for this "Audible" mode is copy and paste an audio file into your Kindle's "Audible" folder rather than its "Music" folder. Then, once you eject the Kindle from your computer connection, you will find the "Audible" folder's new file(s) toward the end of your Home screen display of titles, with the word "audio" to the left of each title line. Just click on the title and you will see easy-to-use listening controls right on your Kindle display.

Later in this chapter we will also take a look at Audible.com itself since, if you are an audible.com subscriber, you will frequently receive offers of *free Audible.com audiobooks* that can be downloaded to your Kindle.

Mozart on Your Kindle: Getting the Most out of Kindle Audio

Let's say that, like many Kindle owners, you are a bit more of a reader than a rocker. Or not. But if you have yet to make much use of the Kindle's audio features, let's walk through a simple and inexpensive process that could provide you with hours of delightful Mozart classics as background music while you read your favorite books or periodicals on your Kindle, all for a grand total of $7.99 and very little expenditure of time. What's not to like about that?

The Kindle MP3 player plays music and podcasts in non-DRM .mp3 format. While it might be nice if you can purchase such content and have it sent wirelessly to your Kindle, audio file sizes and transfer speeds make this unlikely. However, it is easier and cheaper than you may think to purchase reading-friendly background music, transfer it to your Kindle, and start listening.

If you like Wolfgang Amadeus Mozart, start by going to the Amazon page for The 99 Most Essential Mozart Masterpieces (http://amzn.to/eR0LRG), a collection that features hours of wonderful Mozart compositions performed by the world's greatest orchestras and soloists. While it is possible to purchase the individual tracks for 89 cents each, you can spend a total of $7.99 and get all 99 tracks, ranging in length from under two minutes to longer than 15 minutes, just by clicking on the orange "Buy MP3 album with 1-click" button (http://amzn.to/eROLRG) near the upper-right corner of your computer screen. Amazon will begin downloading the album almost immediately, perhaps after asking you to enable the Amazon downloader tool to work on your computer if you have not done so already. Keep track of the destination at which your computer saves the album download, which will usually be in a folder or directory called "Music", associated with your default audio program, such as iTunes or Windows Media Player.

Once the album downloads to your computer, plug your Kindle into your computer via the USB cable. From within your computer's "Finder" or "My Computer" feature, locate the music files that were just downloaded, select the tracks that you want to copy to your Kindle, and pick them up with the **Copy** command. (**Important Note**: Remember that audio files require more storage capacity than text, and *don't overdo it*. I recommend that you choose a dozen or two of the tracks you think you will enjoy the most and copy them rather than trying to store all 99 tracks on your Kindle!)

Next, go to the Kindle folder from your computer's "Finder" or "My Computer" structure, open it, and then open the subfolder called "Music." Use your system's **Paste** command to paste the music tracks into your Kindle's "Music" folder, eject the Kindle from your computer, and you are ready to enjoy some nice background music as you read. Just press Home to go to the Kindle 2 Home screen, press Menu, then use the 5-way or scrollwheel to select "Experimental" and "Play MP3" from the next two menus that appear on your Kindle display.

Listening to Free Audible.com Content on Your Kindle

In addition to the music and podcasts to which you can listen on your Kindle after you store them in your Kindle's "Music" or "Audible" folder via USB connection with your Kindle, you can also purchase and download or transfer Audible.com content and listen to it on your Kindle. If you are already an Audible.com member, you are probably aware that Audible.com files come with better navigational enhancements than the background music files that you may keep in your "Music" folder for Kindle listening, and you probably also know that Audible.com regularly offers

free audiobooks to its members. Also, as of December 2010, when you enter Audible.com for the first time as a Kindle user at http://www.audible.com/kindle you will be invited to get a **free Audible.com book** as a Gold plan customer with **a free month of Audible.com service**.

Once you spring for Audible.com membership -- which begins at $12.46 per month, for an annualized Audible Listener Gold account -- you may be amazed at the hundreds of free audiobooks that are available to you. To browse the possibilities, just go to Audible.com, click on the Advanced Search link (http://bit.ly/eZgEfX) in the upper left corner, and select "**Free**" from the pull-down menu in the Price field.

If you have a latest-generation Kindle with a wi-fi connection, you can now download Audible.com content wirelessly to your Kindle using that connection. You must purchase and download the audiobook first using your computer, but once you've done that, you will be able to find the Audible.com file on your Kindle's listing of Archived Items. Just move the 5-way to the Audible.com title and select it by pressing down to begin the wireless download.

Otherwise, for earlier-generation Kindles, your Kindle, you'll need to use your computer to purchase and download content from Audible.com. Amazon purchased Audible.com around the time of the Kindle launch, so it is fair to expect that Audible.com connectivity for Kindle users may continue be enhanced in the future, but the difficulty that must be overcome both for Audible.com and Amazon MP3 content involves file size and the resulting effect on transfer speed, and it takes a wi-fi connection to address that problem.

For now, purchase your content and use the free Audible Manager software on the site to download it to your computer, then transfer the content to your Kindle's native "Audible" folder using your USB connection. If you are using a Mac, you may not be able to download Audible.com content unless you are using Windows-emulation software. When prompted by Audible Manager to select your listening device's "Audio Format Sound Quality," you can choose 2, 3 or 4 for Kindle compatibility. The best quality, and the largest file size, comes with selection 4 -- whether you choose this option may depend on your download speed and on the file space you have available on your Kindle and, if you are using a Kindle 1, any SD memory cards.

Navigate to http://www.audible.com/kindle and sign up if you have not done so already. Download the Audible Manager software to your computer and re-start your web browser. Connect your Kindle to your computer via USB and "activate" the Kindle as your listening device within Audible Manager. Once you have purchased listening content, you will be able to copy it to your Kindle and listen to it there.

Once you have transferred Audible content to your Kindle you should be able to access it directly from your Home screen with your 5-way, just as you would a Kindle book or other content. Look for a tiny speaker icon next to the Audible.com content.

After you've opened an Audible.com file, just use the onscreen navigation menu to move among your options including Beginning, Previous Section, Next Section, Back 30 seconds, Forward 30 seconds, and a Play/Pause toggle.

You'll have several listening options, including the Kindle's onboard stereo speakers. For a better experience, use the audio jack to the left of the USB slot at the bottom of the Kindle to connect it to a speaker or headset and the sound quality isn't bad. That jack will also work if you have an automobile with an MP3 jack. Further to the right of the Kindle's bottom edge, you will find "down" and "up" volume-control buttons. (Tip: If you don't do a lot of Kindle listening and your first Audible file doesn't seem to be starting for you, make sure that the volume is turned up.)

Between the Chapters, and Just Between Us: How to Contact Kindle Nation

Please feel free contact me any time at kindlenation@gmail.com. I read all email and comments and *try* to respond promptly to polite messages whenever appropriate, often from my other email address, hppress@gmail.com. I also have a Facebook page (http://on.fb.me/fokHHQ) and a Twitter page (http://bit.ly/fhTjbn), but if you want to contact me I check email more often.

Kindle Nation Mailbag. Sometimes, if I think the topic of an email message or comment will be of interest to a wider group of the citizens of Kindle Nation, I'll include the message and my response in a From the Kindle Nation Mailbag post, but I only use first names there. If you don't want your message included, be sure to let me know!

Post Comments. I also welcome comments in response to any Kindle Nation post, but I do moderate comments and I try not to allow spam or incivility, especially when it is unsigned. There are plenty of places where spam and incivility are welcome, but life is too short for this to be one of them.

Sponsorships. We do not allow Google Ads or similar advertising on Kindle Nation and you'll never see advertising or spam for Viagra, get-rich-quick schemes, or similar items on our blog. Instead, we accept sponsorships for Kindle ebooks, blogs, periodicals, and accessories as part of our ongoing effort to connect readers and writers through Kindle while also defraying our expenses. If you are an author, publisher, or accessory vendor and you are interested in learning more about sponsorship, there's more info here (http://bit.ly/ecMhY8).

Ch 10: Ten Reasons the New Kindle 3 or Kindle Wi-Fi Is a Must if You Love to Read ... And a Few Minor Drawbacks

Back on July 28, after testing the new $189 Kindle 3G (http://amzn.to/g2OXBL) and the $139 Kindle Wi-Fi (http://amzn.to/fOdBW7) for half an hour, I gave the newest Amazon device a pretty strong "Wow". I've been using Kindles now for three years and have been through every model and every Kindle App but one, but it was clear to me almost immediately that Amazon had done some wonderful things with the new release, all while maintaining its new $189 price point. More about that price point later, of course, but the initial thing to say about the $189 price point is that, while it may not be quite the equivalent of an impulse buy for electronics, it is 53 percent lower than the price that thousands of us paid for a much more basic Kindle 1 back in 2007 and 2008.

Now that I have been using a Kindle 3 nearly non-stop for the past five days, thanks to my receipt of a "review" Kindle from Amazon last Wednesday, I am prepared to be much more articulate about it.

This Kindle 3G (http://amzn.to/g2OXBL) is a Triple Wow. Five Stars. Two Thumbs Up. And, because Amazon stays true to its core vision of catalog, convenience and connectivity for the Kindle, it is by far the best ebook reader ever made. For now, and probably for the rest of 2010, at the least.

Naturally, as with any other kind of technology, there will be serious people who want no part of it.

Some will hate it because it is "only" an ebook reader. It does astonishingly well with audio in several useful and attractive ways, but it does not support video or animation or sophisticated gaming and its lack of color will rule it out for some textbooks, art books, comic books, manga and other illustrated or design-intensive books.

Some will hate it because it doesn't have a touch screen. I use an iPad or iPod Touch frequently enough so that my muscle memory sometimes gets ahead of me and I find myself tapping my Kindle screen. And I doubt I will ever get used to any of the Kindle keyboards, so there are times when I would love to be able to add annotations to my Kindle content with a stylus. And speaking of input, I just don't understand why the keyboard can't have a number row -- there's room for it! But these are minor complaints. When it comes to actual reading of a novel or any text-intensive book, article, newspaper, magazine, or blog, the Kindle 3 provides an exquisite experience.

Some will miss the configuration of buttons and bars on earlier Kindles, as the new Kindle 3 places the Menu, Home, and Back buttons adjacent to the keyboards and transforms the 5-way into something more trackpad-like, but for most of us all of this will be old hat within a week.

Some will want to avoid doing anything to hasten the inevitable transition in publishing technologies, but their fingers in the dike of change will be seriously overmatched as the number of devices being used as ebook readers soars past 10 million in 2010, 20 million in 2011 and 60 million by 2015.

Some will want to stay with print books and their favorite brick-and-mortar bookstores, but unfortunately over the course of the next five years the availability of these pleasures will decline dramatically, and by the end of the decade there will be far fewer print books manufactured and even fewer places to buy them.

Some will be impatient, as I am, for Amazon to put on some speed with respect to the kind of true internationalization for the entire Kindle platform that would be signified with more alphabets (whether or not they are supported for the Kindle 3 has been handled somewhat mysteriously), more in-country stores, translation dictionaries, and a much wider selection in languages other than English, but the Kindle 3 may indeed be the hardware device that opens the doors to all of this, and there have been plentiful rumors lately of Kindle launches in China and elsewhere.

Some will continue their call for Amazon to open up the Kindle to one or more of the variations on the highly Balkanized ePub format, or to library ebooks, or other "open" formats, but adherents of such moves have demonstrated little support among Kindle owners and do not seem to understand Amazon's need to conduct itself as a business.

Some will be content to stick with devices they own already, including the Kindle 1 and Kindle 2 as well as other ebook readers, but even before the first Kindle 3 order has been filled, our most recent Kindle Nation survey (http://conta.cc/gv5b4V) suggests strongly that nearly one-fourth of existing Kindle owners plan to upgrade to a Kindle 3 or Kindle 3 Wi-Fi Only before the end of 2010.

So, in enumerating the top ten reasons why the Kindle 3 is a "must-have" reading device for me, for you, and for millions of other people who love to read, let's start there:

10. At $139 and $189, the Kindle 3 is the Best Value Proposition Ever for an eBook Reader

There aren't as many readers as there are people who talk on the phone or drive cars, so there may never be as many Kindles as there are cell phones or automobiles, but that doesn't mean they won't be ubiquitous in the circles in which you travel. The combined force of the Kindle 3's $139 and $189 price points and the superior reading experience that it provides means that most of the people you know will own a Kindle within two years, and most of the people you consider smart will own a Kindle *this* year. And the fact that Amazon is selling a unit that is identical in every respect except 3G wi-fi connectivity for just $139 means that most of those smart people will be buying multiple wi-fi -only Kindle 3s for their children, grandchildren and others on their gift lists this holiday season. The hardest work I'll be doing in organizing my 2010 holiday list is trying to figure out who might already be getting a Kindle 3 from someone else, and which people spend so much time in wi-fi settings that they might not need the 3G model.

The other hard part -- and this may require the services of a certified swami -- will involve figuring out when I need to place my orders to ensure that Amazon will be able to deliver my gift Kindles in time for the holidays. Although Amazon cemented the Kindle's current dominant position among ebook readers by never running out of Kindles during the 2009 holiday season, that stands in stark contrast to the company's grinchy experience during the 2007 and 2008 holiday seasons, when there were no Kindles to ship in either year. Pre-order delivery dates for both Kindle 3 models have been getting pushed back throughout the entire month of August, and the most worrisome indication is that the length of the shipping delay noted on the Kindle buying pages has been lengthening.

This obviously indicates very high demand (unless, call me a cynic for raising the issue, it is all a marketing gimmick?), and it may also inspire resellers to place bulk orders in order to take advantage of impatience premiums, high demand, and arbitrage profits on third-party seller sites including eBay, Craigslist, and Amazon's own Marketplace. If an authorized retailer like Target quickly runs out of Kindle 3 units when it receives its first supply in September, it will be a clear sign that we may see stock-out situations on and off through the end of 2010.

Of course, if prices of $189 and $139 alone were sufficient reason for people to buy a Kindle, the Kindle's share of the market might be split more democratically with devices like the Nook and Sony's various offerings. But that's not what's happening. Amazon has hit the sweet spot by offering all of the other benefits that fill out this top ten list at these prices, and as a result the Kindle's current installed base of about 4.5 million Kindles will swell to well over 7 million by the end of this year. In addition to the million Kindle 3s that Amazon will sell to current Kindle owners and over a million Kindle 3s that will become their new owners' first ebook readers, there will be at least half a million Kindle 3s sold this year to people who started out reading Kindle content on other devices like the iPad, iPod Touch, BlackBerry, Android, Mac or PC. Every other device with a freely downloadable Kindle App, and every ebook added to the relentlessly growing Kindle catalog, becomes a kind of Trojan Horse that will lead to more content sales and ultimately to more hardware and accessory sales for Amazon in the future.

These days, when anyone who enjoys reading tells me he doesn't want a Kindle, my answer is simple: "That's only because you haven't tried one." But if Amazon can do a better job of keeping the Kindle 3 in stock, the company has a friction-free solution to that problem in its free "test drive" policy for Kindles and other products: you can buy any Kindle and use it for up to 30 days, then return it for a full refund with no questions asked. My guess is that there will be very few Kindle 3 returns.

Now that Amazon has released a remarkably full-featured Kindle Wi-Fi model (http://amzn.to/gTeNS2) for just $139, the $50 price differential between that model and the $189 Kindle 3G places an elegant value-proposition accent on the Kindle's wireless connectivity. If you think that either of these Kindles is worth $139 as an ereader, that just leaves this question: would you pay $50 one time, with no monthly fees or AT+T contracts, for wireless connectivity that would allow you to check email, scores, stocks, weather and any text-intensive website from just about anywhere for the rest of your life? I've exaggerated the proposition here, because there's a good chance you will outlive your Kindle, but you get the idea.

By the way, if you frequently send personal documents and free ebooks from other sources to your Kindle, the availability of wi-fi on both Kindle 3 models will save you money on those pesky wireless transfer charges. And if those personal documents come in the form of PDFs, the Kindle 3 PDF reading experience is the best yet for a Kindle, with support for password protection, highlighting and annotations, and multiple contrast settings.

9. An Enhanced "Webkit" Web Browser Makes the Kindle's Free Wireless Internet Connectivity Better Than Ever

One of the things that impressed me about the Kindle from the first days of the Kindle 1 was the fact that it came with free "lifetime" wireless web connectivity with no contract, no monthly fees, and -- did we say it was free? -- no cost ever. Of course that was great for accessing the Kindle Store and downloading books in less than 60 seconds, but it also meant that no matter where I was -- with very few out-of-range exceptions -- I could check my email or the Red Sox score or any text-intensive web page. The drawback, of course, was that the browser was pretty clunky and web pages usually took forever to load.

Many of us wondered back in 2007 and 2008 if Amazon would eventually abandon or begin charging for the web access. Instead, the Kindle 3 makes it clear that the free wireless internet connectivity is here to stay and makes it more valuable than ever by adding a new web browser based on WebKit (http://webkit.org/), the open-sourced Web browser engine that is also the basis for ... are you ready for this? ... Apple's Safari web browser. Don't get me wrong: pages are still a little slow to load, like benign but occasionally annoying intruders from the age of dial-up, but the combination of the new browser and the much-improved Kindle 3 display provide a *faster, more useful, vastly improved but still absolutely free web browser* that serves up complex web pages far better than the browser on earlier Kindles.

The new browser also includes a **new Article Mode feature** that simplifies most web pages to text-based content reading by omitting the usual sidebar stuff and other extraneous material. Article Mode's purpose is similar in one respect to that of Instapaper, but Instapaper's superb usefulness for adding articles on the fly to a tidy daily digest that renders beautifully on any Kindle remains unmatched in my view.

The $189 Kindle 3 provides for an **automatic toggle between 3G wireless and wi-fi connectivity** that makes use of the best, fastest network available once you've synched it up with your home, office, or local coffee shop's wi-fi interface. The web browser and all other wireless functionality were especially fast when using my home wi-fi connection.

Parenthetically, one thing I like about the new web browser is that it makes it easy to go to various pages on Amazon's website and place an order, change a setting on my Manage Your Kindle page, or read content there, so that Amazon is finally beginning to deliver on the promise that the Kindle holds as a portal to direct Amazon ordering.

For Kindle Nation Daily readers, this will make it easier than ever to get the most out of a Kindle subcription to this blog (http://amzn.to/e9oXQo) by clicking, for example, on a title in our daily Free Book Alert and placing an order seamlessly on the Amazon website right from your Kindle. I placed such orders twice this weekend while connected via my home wi-fi and in both cases the ebook was downloaded to my Kindle Home screen 4 seconds after I clicked the "Buy" button.

8. Text-to-Speech and Voice Guide

Whether you are visually impaired or just someone, like me, who likes to listen to some kinds of Kindle content at the gym, in the car, or while falling asleep, the Kindle's audio accessibility features keep getting more and more useful. The text-to-speech voices are a little less robotic than they were at launch in February 2009, and their command of vocabulary and proper nouns has improved significantly, even allowing for the occasional amusing mispronunciation and their annoying habit of reading certain fairly common words as state name abbreviations, especially when they come at the end of a sentence: "even in the crowd, she was hard to Mississippi." Kindle text-to-speech may not be a great way to listen to Shakespeare, but for newspaper, magazine, and blog articles and some nonfiction it can be a terrific way to expand one's reading time and reach, and with over half a million text-to-speech enabled Kindle books, that has to be true ten times over for many visually impaired readers.

The Kindle remains the only ebook reader with text-to-speech, and now the value of text-to-speech has been augmented with new *voice-guided text-to-speech enabled menus* that allow us to navigate on the Kindle without having to read menu options or content listings and item descriptions on the home screen. The new Voice Guide, audible menuing feature handles all of that with spoken menus, selectable items, and descriptions.

For example, when you open a book, Kindle speaks your current location and how far you've read. Voice Guide can be turned on or off in a snap by pressing the Menu button from the Home screen, using the 5-way to underline and select "Settings", pressing Next Page to go to Page 2 of

Settings, and using the 5-way to underline and select "turn on" or "turn off" next to the "Voice Guide" setting. Once Voice Guide is set, it can be left on indefinitely, and the result is a far more accessible ebook reader that has won the endorsement of the National Federation of the Blind (http://bit.ly/gW5TQP). However, Amazon could make this combination of accessibility features far more useful by simplifying the text-to-speech command process once the Voice Guide feature is turned on.

7. The Kindle 3 is a Direct-Download Media Player for Audible.com Audiobooks, and Perhaps for Other Audio Content in the Future

Now that Amazon has perfected the Kindle as a delivery device for its growing ebook catalog, it is branching out. With the Kindle 3, according to the new Kindle 3 User's Guide, you will be able purchase, transfer, and play Audible.com audiobooks from Amazon and have them delivered wirelessly to your Kindle via any wi-fi connection, without having to go through the hassle of connecting to a computer via USB. The new Kindle 3 User's Guide says that these Audible listings will be available right in the Kindle Store, and it is fair to assume that this availability will be rolled out at some point between now and the Kindle 3 ship date.

Audible.com audiobooks have played nicely with the Kindle in the past, but in the past you have always had to download them to your computer first, and then transfer them to your Kindle via USB cable. Now that Amazon is using wi-fi connectivity to make the Kindle 3 a seamless delivery device for its Audible.com subsidiary, it may be just a matter of time before Amazon adds similar purchase, download, and playback functionality for its vast catalog of MP3 music and other audio files. In that connection, let me say that I played Travie McCoy's "Billionaire", one of my 12-year-old son Danny's favorite songs (he has has the PG-13 version on his iPod Touch), side by side on the Kindle 3 and the iPad this week and found no easily discernible difference in audio quality.

I asked an Amazon spokesperson what I could expect in terms of launch announcements and related developments for the new Kindle 3 Audible.com functionality, and she answered with the first two words Amazon teaches to its future PR staffers at when they are hatched: "Stay tuned." And that, I am sure, is also the answer I would have received if I had asked any Amazon plans to open up its music store to direct Kindle downloads or to add Kindle 3 features that would make use of the mysterious microphone that sits unused on the bottom edge of the new Kindle.

6. The Kindle 3 is the Greatest Travel Companion Ever

Amazon has doubled the storage capacity of the Kindle 3 so that at 4 GB it holds up to 3,500 ebooks, with unlimited additional room for your archived purchases in Amazon's cloud, so every serious reader's travel baggage just got lighter. You can read on the Kindle anywhere, of course. The lighted Kindle cover will keep you from ever having to reach up again for one of those terrible airline lights on a night flight, and of course you know that you can read it on the beach and when you finish one great beach novel you can look up the sequel, download it, and begin reading it within 60 seconds without leaving the beach. Please don't tell Betty I said this, but those features alone might make the Kindle 3 the greatest travel companion ever.

But of course that's not all. With the Kindle 3's improved web functionality, it can also help you decide where to go for dinner, show you what's playing at local theaters, or let you check your email. All without monthly charges, contracts, or roaming fees, from just about anywhere.

The combination of global 3G and wi-fi will be especially valuable to travelers who will be able to add and update Kindle content and even check web pages on the road without the need for a USB connection to a computer or, in over 100 countries, those pesky international wireless charges. For international customers, Amazon has been adding free web browsing gradually on a country-by-country basis around the world, so that these Kindle 3 features are likely to become a greater and greater selling point worldwide.

5. The Lighted Leather Kindle Cover is the Best eBook Reader Accessory Ever, Even at $59.99

One of the coolest things I experienced in my test drive of the new Kindle 3 (http://amzn.to/h8Rfz3) is something that, admittedly, does not come standard in the Kindle box. The new Kindle Lighted Leather Cover (http://amzn.to/h9Vn4E) combines some very forward technologies with great Moleskine-like style in a choice of seven colors. There's even an elastic strap to keep the cover firmly closed (or conveniently opened and folded back). The price is $59.99, but you will effectively be buying two Kindle accessories in one, and you'll never need batteries. All seven covers include an integrated, retractable LED reading light that hides away into the cover when not in use. It lights the entire Kindle display without glare and draws its power directly from the Kindle's battery through the new gold-plated conductive hinges that connect the Kindle to the cover. Between this lighted cover and the new quieter* page turns, reading may be moving dramatically, even ominously, up the list of the most fun things you can do in bed.

The new lighted cover works with both new Kindle 3 models, the Kindle 3G (http://amzn.to/h8Rfz3) and the Kindle Wi-Fi (http://amzn.to/hs1ie7), but please don't order it as a Kindle 1 or Kindle 2 accessory, because it doesn't fit those larger earlier models. Here are the color choices:

Kindle Lighted Leather Cover, Black (Fits 6" Display, Latest Generation Kindle) - http://amzn.to/blackcover

Kindle Lighted Leather Cover, Chocolate Brown (Fits 6"
Display, Latest Generation Kindle) -
http://amzn.to/browncover

Kindle Lighted Leather Cover, Burnt Orange (Fits 6" Display,
Latest Generation Kindle) - http://amzn.to/orangecover

Kindle Lighted Leather Cover, Apple Green (Fits 6" Display,
Latest Generation Kindle) - http://amzn.to/greencover

Kindle Lighted Leather Cover, Burgundy Red (Fits 6"
Display, Latest Generation Kindle) -
http://amzn.to/redcover

Kindle Lighted Leather Cover, Steel Blue (Fits 6" Display,
Latest Generation Kindle) - http://amzn.to/bluecover

Kindle Lighted Leather Cover, Hot Pink (Fits 6" Display,
Latest Generation Kindle) - http://amzn.to/pinkcover

If you have no use for the reading light, you can get
essentially the same cover *without* the retractable light for
$25 less, in the same array of colors
(http://amzn.to/nolight).

*The Kindle 3's Next Page and Previous Page bars are much
narrower and a little less noisy with less of a bounce-back
click than the wider buttons on the Kindle 2. They take a

little getting used to if you are trying to find the quietest way of tapping them so as not to wake or annoy your partner while reading in bed, but once you get the hang of it they are definitely quieter.

4. WhisperSynch Interoperability and Free Kindle App Downloads Mean Never Having to Be Without Your Reading

With respect to reading, my Kindle is the mother ship. This has been true with every Kindle I have owned, but the Kindle 3 reading experience is so terrific that I would seldom choose to read on another device. Nevertheless, there are plenty of people using the "No Kindle Required" approach with freely downloadable Kindle apps for other devices and there are even times when for one reason or another I am without my Kindle when I want to read a few pages of a Kindle book. For all of us, Amazon makes this a shockingly easy, friction-free experience. It doesn't take a bit of work. How great a feature is this capacity to move seamlessly from one Kindle-compatible device to another?

Well, for comparison's sake, can we discuss iTunes for a moment? Members of my immediate household own 1 iPad and 3 iPod Touch units. Each of them is connected to the same Apple iTunes account. We've paid the iTunes Store for hundreds of songs, perhaps thousands. We've spent hours saving other digital files from CDs we had purchased over the past couple of decades, strictly for our own personal use, and there are no pirated songs or files on any of our various devices and hard drives.

So why is it that my son and I can't access each other's iTunes songs, all paid for with the same account? And why, whenever we're getting ready for a road trip where we might have an opportunity to listen to some music, does the preparation always seem to include a rather nudgy and painstaking process of getting the right stuff to synch up on the right devices without overwhelming storage space with free sample episodes of Friday Night Lights that I apparently made the mistake of downloading to my iTunes account in some earlier decade? And why does Apple insist on prompting me to download a new iTunes software update about every third time I log onto iTunes? And why, if I say yes, does the process slow down my 2009 iMac to a near crawl for the next 20 minutes?

Can't this stuff be done in the background? Has Apple not heard of the cloud? My point here, of course, is not to complain about Apple so much as it is to say that, for the Kindle platform and the various Kindle apps, Amazon has nailed this stuff. And it is important, whether it comes up ten times a week or once a year.

3. The Best eBook Catalog Ever, Until Tomorrow, When It Will Be Better Still

You may prefer to read ebooks on some other device, but if you are interested in a wide selection at the best available prices, most of the ebooks you are likely to be reading are going to come from the Kindle Store. Although various retailers have tried to play a numbers game and puff up their catalog statistics with duplicative public domain fluff, no other ebook store comes close to the Kindle Store's selection of over 650,000 commercially available ebooks, 136 newspapers, 68 magazines and journals, and nearly 10,000 blogs. Amazon and various third parties also make it a snap to find and download over a million other free books.

Amazon has made it very easy to buy, download, and read all of those ebooks on other devices owned by millions of people, and the company says that about 20 percent of the ebooks sold in the Kindle Store are downloaded to those other devices. But the vast majority of those who have compared reading on the Kindle with reading on an iPad, iPhone, iPod Touch, BlackBerry, PC, or Mac prefer the Kindle as the superior reading experience. Those stated preferences, of course, have been based on comparisons involving earlier Kindle models. My own view of the difference between the Kindle 3 and the Kindle 2 is that the Kindle 3 provides at least twice as good an overall experience, for the same or a significantly lower price than what owners paid for the Kindle 2. Case closed.

2. With Better Contrast in a Smaller, Lighter, Faster Kindle with Improved Battery Life, Amazon Continues to Demonstrate its Commitment to Progressive Improvement, Enhancement, and Efficiency of the Kindle

The most dramatic of these incremental changes, for me, involves the same Pearl e-ink technology found in the relatively new Kindle DX Graphite unit, providing the basis for Amazon's claims of *50 percent better contrast* due to lighter background and a choice of three darker, clearer, sharper fonts. Frankly, after reading for a while with the Kindle 3 (or, for that matter, the Kindle DX Graphite unit) and then going back to my Kindle 2, I was surprised that I hadn't complained much about poor contrast on the Kindle 2.

Although the Kindle 3 provides the same size display, at 6 inches, as the Kindle 2, it is housed in hardware that is significantly smaller in all three dimensions, so that the mass of the Kindle 3 is *21 percent smaller* and, at just 8.7 ounces, *15 percent lighter* than the Kindle 2, and the WiFi-only unit measures out the same but is a little lighter still. You also get, in either unit:

a 20 percent faster screen refresh or page-turn speed;

a choice of two case colors, the classic white or the new contrast-enhancing graphite case that I've found very attractive with the new Kindle DX;

more than double the storage space from the 1,500 books accomodated by the Kindle 2 to a 3,500-book capacity that equals that of the Kindle DX; and

The longest battery life between charges yet for a Kindle or any other ereader, according to Amazon: one month with the wireless turned off, and 10 days with the wireless turned on. The time between charges can be lengthened if you use wi-fi most of the time, or shortened by factors as use of the Kindle's audio features.

Although the Kindle 3 display is no larger than that on the Kindle 1 or Kindle 2, the display is used more efficiently so that one sees more text on each page.

1. The Kindle 3 is the Least Expensive and Most User-Friendly Way Ever to Build a Permanent Library

If you love to read, you've got to have a Kindle 3 (http://amzn.to/g2OXBL). Libraries and gifts and used books notwithstanding, most adults who love to read have become accustomed to spending over $20 a month on books, some of us much more. Whether or not the Kindle 3 actually saves you back the $189 or $139 that you pay for it will depend on your individual book buying behavior, but chances are good that you will read more, spend less, and enjoy your reading more with a Kindle 3. That's my experience and judgment, and it has been the experience already of thousands of Kindle 1, Kindle 2, and Kindle DX owners with those devices. With the Kindle 3, that experience is going to be even better.

Between the Chapters, and Just Between Us: Kindle Periodicals and Your Battery

Regardless of whether your Kindle is using 3G or wi-fi for wireless connectivity, you can extend the time before you will need to recharge your Kindle battery by turning the wireless off when you aren't using it. All well and good, but keep in mind that you will need to turn your wireless on to receive newspapers, magazines, blog posts and ebooks on your Kindle. The on-off switch for your Kindle wireless is accessible at the top of the Home Menu.

Ch 11: The Politics of "Free" Books In the Age of the Kindle

Let's keep this brief. It is certainly neither my assumption nor my expectation that you are here out of interest in the politics of the ebook industry or "the ebook movement" or "the Kindle revolution." But if you are an avid reader, you are likely to be affected by these issues in one way or another. But rather than go on at great length about these issues myself, I will suggest a few very basic definitions and point in the direction of some material that I believe would be helpful for those who wish to read further.

When people talk about "free" digital content such as ebooks, digital music files, and video content, they are usually speaking of one or both of two kinds of "free", either:

• Content that is free of charge, zero-priced, or available for the taking through a legal download or other transaction; or

• Content that is free of digital restrictions, such as the Digital Rights Management (DRM) restrictions placed on many Kindle books by Amazon or publishers or other ebook retailers, that might limit one from making various non-commercial uses of that content.

Zero-Priced Content

The chapters you have been reading in this ebook have been all about various entirely legal ways of acquiring content at zero price, and we have already seen how free books have come increasingly to dominate the top Kindle Store bestsellers. When books are free, the content is free because either:

• it is no longer protected by copyright due to its publication date (http://bit.ly/hsvS0j), and therefore in the "public domain" (http://bit.ly/hsvS0j), (although there is also a long and perfectly respectable history of publishers and retailers selling public domain books for a profit);

• it has been explicitly released by the author or rightsholder(s) to the public domain through a Creative Commons (http://bit.ly/dXhXpG) license or some similar device; or

• its price has been set at free or zero either temporarily or permanently by its author, publisher, or retailer in order to make it more widely available, as a promotional strategy for itself or other works, or as a "loss leader" (http://bit.ly/lossleader), or in order to sell ebook devices, or in order to generate ancillary revenue with an alternative model in which the content drives traffic, affiliate fees (http://bit.ly/gDu2CX), or advertising revenue.

Issues related to free ebooks, music, and newspaper content have exploded over the past two decades with the explosive growth in popularity of the web. The Long Tail (http://amzn.to/gMIH16) author Chris Anderson has been a leading herald of a downward price spiral toward free content, most recently in his book Free: The Future of a Radical Price (http://amzn.to/freefuture), which at this writing is priced at $9.49 in the Kindle Store after an initial period as a free book:

 Free by Chris Anderson (**Kindle Edition** - Jul 7, 2009) - **Kindle Book**
Buy: **$0.00**
Auto-delivered wirelessly
★★★★☆ (32)
Other Editions: Hardcover

Whether this "downward price spiral toward free content" is seen as a viral marketing strategy or as the inevitable consequence of the spread of new technologies, it is obviously unsustainable at its final, absolute level. Whether one thinks of Anderson or me or anyone else who writes a book entitled *Free* or *Kindle Free for All* as authors, as content providers, or as search engine and advertising magnets, either we must have ways of being paid for our work or we will have to find other work. Author Malcolm Gladwell has offered an uneven critique of the free content approach in his New Yorker review of Anderson's book at http://bit.ly/Gladwell-on-Free.

While controversies over the apparent death spiral of a newsprint-based newspaper industry and the rise, fall, and rise of Napster and various business ventures which followed it have made us all a little more knowledgeable and a lot more opinionated about free content and its attendant issues, it is important to remember that there are special issues in each category there that should keep us from lumping all forms of free content together. With some exceptions, ebooks do not suffer because they contain information that readers would otherwise get for free online, and with even fewer exceptions, ebooks cannot be seen as loss leaders to inspire readers to buy concert tickets for the next live show by Stephenie Meyer or James Patterson.

DRM and DRM-Free Content

We discussed Digital Rights Management (DRM) briefly in the context of digital music such as MP3 files back in Chapter 9, but it is an equally gnarly issue in the context of the Kindle specifically and ebooks in general. The much-ballyhooed and often confused July 2009 "the Kindle ate my homework" (http://cnet.co/atehomework) controversy over Amazon's removal of two copyright-violating George Orwell novels from customers' Kindles put a spotlight on our worst fears about DRM.

Amazon's motivation for its DRM policy may well be based on a business need to protect publishers' copyright interests as a necessary basis for their participating, but one does not need to sport a tinfoil hat to realize that DRM can become a more ominous restriction in a world where the Kindle's Whispernet wireless connectivity is a two-way street.

In essence, the fact that most Kindle editions currently come with DRM combined with Amazon's nearly constant wireless access to the Kindle hardware that we have purchased gave Amazon the power to go back into our Kindles to grab and delete not only the books that customers had purchased and downloaded, but also the annotations, highlights, and highlights that they had made in the text. To the shock and outrage of many, that is just the "Orwellian" step that Amazon took when it discovered that two of the Orwell novels being offered in the Kindle Store were in copyright violation. Even for those of us who understand and sympathize with the importance of protecting the Orwell copyright interest, there seemed little excuse for the fact that Amazon acted surreptitiously, without warning, and without providing customers with the chance to download an alternative copyright-compliant version and synch up annotations.

To his credit, Amazon founder and CEO Jeff Bezos offered an exemplary apology for the company's actions (http://bit.ly/BezosApology). That has not kept some customers from filing or contemplating class action lawsuits over the matter, and it will continue to fester as part of a broader set of concerns and campaigns around DRM until, at the very least, Amazon brings greater light and clarity to the DRM issue and guarantees that it will not repeat such actions in the future.

As I have written elsewhere, I believe it is likely that Amazon will eventually follow in the footsteps of Apple, iTunes, and the iPod with respect to DRM by loosening DRM restrictions on Kindle editions in the future, perhaps at a pricing premium (http://bit.ly/WindwalkeronKindleDRM1). But such predictions from me fall far short of a guarantee, and as technology blogger Mike Elgan pointed out in an interview with Len Edgerly on his The Kindle Chronicles 53 podcast (http://bit.ly/k-chronicles), DRM is very much in Amazon's business interest now in exactly the same way it was, at first, in Apple's interest, because "the biggest buyers of books actually invest their time and money into a format which is Amazon's format..."

"The way [Apple] set up the iTunes store and the way they did DRM and all that stuff.... After a year or two went by and Apple became the number one player people had invested enormous amounts of money in buying songs, and to move to a competitive player was kind of out of the question for a lot of people because they couldn't just abandon a thousand dollars worth of investment in songs.... [So, since] the top five per cent of book buyers buy 20 per cent of the books ... the biggest buyers of books ... those heavy duty users .. those are the people who Amazon has essentially captured into its format [with the Kindle]."

The reality, of course, is that we'll have to wait and see. The practices and initiatives of readers, authors, publishers, retailers and perhaps even courts and government agencies will play out in ways that are probably too complex to predict at the present time, and even Amazon itself will have to share the tiller as we navigate these rapids. Meanwhile, for an excellent introduction to DRM issues as they relate to ebooks, I strongly recommend DRM: A TeleRead Primer (http://bit.ly/drm-primer), posted on December 6, 2008 by Chris Meadows.

Between the Chapters, and Just Between Us: The Future of Free in the Kindle Store

Do you like free books? I thought so.

Did you know that there are hundreds of Kindle authors who want to make more Kindle books free but are -- as of late 2010 -- prohibited from doing so?

That's right. Large publishers use free Kindle books -- often with one book in an author's series, or that sort of thing -- to help market authors' other books. There's a good chance that your Kindle library already contains some of these books or, if you are new to the Kindle, that it soon will.

Unfortunately, while Amazon has done great things to level the playing field for indie authors in other ways, it is still impossible for the authors and publishers who use the Kindle Digital Text Platform to help connect with readers by occasionally offering free Kindle titles.

Don't get me wrong. The last thing I want to see is a great cluttering of the Kindle Store. But it would be easy for

Amazon to establish clear and consistent limitations on zero-priced book promotions and then to allow such promotions across the board. It would mean more free books for customers, but if handled properly it would also lead to more paid book sales for authors, for publishers, and for Amazon.

For instance, an author or publisher with anywhere from 3 to 200 titles might be allowed one free promotion at any given time, and at higher levels no more than 1% of their active catalog could be offered free. The other titles would have to be enrolled in the Kindle Store's 70% royalty program, and other appropriate requirements could be added.

If you'd like to see that kind of innovation to give small presses and indie authors a fair chance to compete with the agency model publishers, I hope you'll consider sending an email message to kindle-feedback@amazon.com, with a cc to:

dtp-feedback@amazon.com and kindlenation@gmail.com. Maybe it will result in a real free for all!

Ch 12: The Myth of the Kindle's "Standard" $9.99 Price, the Agency Model, and the ABCs of Kindle Store Pricing

If you were to rely strictly on the mainstream media coverage of Kindle-related news for your information, you could not be faulted for believing that most Kindle books are priced at $9.99.

In fact, fewer than one out of every ten Kindle Store books -- 9.5% as of December 2010 -- are priced at $9.99. The vast majority of the rest -- 75% of all 785,000 Kindle editions -- are priced *below* $9.99, including over 99,000 titles that are priced anywhere from 99 cents down to "Free."

Part of the cause of this confusion comes from Amazon itself, since the company's marketing efforts for the Kindle have sometimes focused on the $9.99 price point as if it were a standard price. But as some "agency model" publishers have formed an alliance of questionable legality with Apple mogul Steve Jobs to try to drive ebook prices higher, Amazon itself has countered by bringing a wide array of authors and publishers directly into the Kindle Store and by adjusting its royalty structure to allow authors to earn better royalties on ebooks priced from $2.99 to $4.99 than they previously earned on paperbacks priced in the $7.99 to $15 range.

Every few weeks we do a statistical analysis of prices in the Kindle Store with a view toward answering the following questions and seeing where the trendlines emerge:

1.   What's the overall size of the Kindle catalog and how does it compare with that of other ebook retailers?

2.   How successful has Amazon been in herding prices into its preferred corral between $2.99 and $9.99, inclusive?

3.   How successful have the big agency model publishers and their Black Knight, Apple anti-reading crusader Steve Jobs, been in raising Kindle Store prices above $10?

4.   Has there been a significant change in the title count for Kindle books priced under $2.99 since Amazon began paying a 70 percent royalty for books in the $2.99 to $9.99 range?

5.   Overall, are ebook prices going up or down or staying about the same?

6.   Are their changes in the price composition of the Kindle Store's key bestseller list, the Top 100 Paid Books?

7.   Are there any noteworthy trends with respect to free books in the Kindle Store?

As of early December 2010, here's what we found:

1.   **Overall Catalog Count**. There are currently 769,766 books in the Kindle Store, which means that the count has grown by about 12,000 books a month since we last checked in in early September. It also means that the Kindle Store catalog has almost doubled from its level of about 410,000 books when Apple announced the iPad and the iBooks Store in late January. The iBooks Store launched with 60,000 titles in early April and has grown to something in the range of 70,000 titles in the seven intermittent months. We'd ask "what's up with that," but we don't want to do anything to distract Steve Jobs or interfere with his sense of balance   as   he   stands   on   Amazon's   shoulders (http://nyr.kr/steve-j) and holds onto the iBooks Store's reported 6 percent market share.

2. **Titles in the $2.99-$9.99 Range**. You'd have to say that Amazon is doing reasonably well at herding prices into its preferred price range of $2.99 to $9.99, but it could do a lot better. The number of titles priced in that range is at 65 percent, the highest it has been at any time this year. It hovered around 51 percent early this year, then jumped to 57 percent in the Spring after Amazon announced that books in that range would qualify for an increase from 35 to 70 percent royalties (net of delivery costs). The percentage grew to 64 percent once the royalty change took effect in early Summer, and has grown by less than 1 percent since. However, it is worth pointing out that titles priced at exactly $2.99 have seen the most significant overall increase of any Kindle Store price point, growing from 18,804 to 29,042 since September 5.

3. **Agency Model Pricing Above $10**. The Agency Model, if you've come a little late to this party, is a baldly anti-consumer price-fixing conspiracy (I wish I didn't have to use that word, but sometimes a conspiracy is just that, a conspiracy) that was hatched at the beginning of 2010 by some combination of Steve Jobs and executives of five of the Big Six publishers, with Random House abstaining. The

stated goal was to mandate retail prices for Kindle books, and all other ebooks under the agency model publishers' control, at levels that would be 30 to 50 percent higher than the $9.99 price that Amazon had previously set for Kindle Store new releases. The only slightly less obvious unstated goal was to slow the migration of readers from print books to ebooks. (Retailers had always had the freedom to discount as they saw fit from the publishers' suggested retail prices in the past, and Amazon had in fact been selling many Kindle titles as loss leaders.) Since the Agency Model went into effect on April Fool's Day, the percentage of the Kindle Store catalog priced in agency-model heaven at $10 and up has fallen from 21.7% to 19.2% on May 22, 18.8% on June 14, 18.1% on July 18, 16% on September 5, and 15.3% today. So what's really going on? Clearly, some agency model publishers are breaking ranks whenever they can in order to actually sell some books. Too many books that readers actually want to buy, of course, are still being priced at silly levels, including many at levels that are within a few cents of print editions, or even higher than print editions. But it is also clear from anecdotal evidence that the large traditional dinosaur publishers' overall share of the ebook market -- both in terms of share-of-catalog and share-of-sales -- is declining as growing numbers of authors go direct-to-Kindle or publish through more innovative companies like RosettaBooks, Open Road Media, AmazonEncore, and hundreds (at least) of other indie publishers.

4. **Books Priced Under $2.99**. This may just be some kind of minor blip that could involve books from a particular publisher being allowed in through a crack under the door, but while there hasn't been any major sea change in the total number of books priced under $2.99 (20.8 percent, up from 20.6 percent three months ago), there is a noticeable bump in the percentage of books priced between a penny and 98 cents. That group, at price points which are not accessible to authors and publishers who use the Kindle Digital Text Platform, has more than doubled from 6,914 to 14,688 since September 5. There may not be much money in it for the rightsholders given the low prices, and there has not been any corresponding increase in the number of books priced at exactly 99 cents, but it is clear that books at these prices continue to have a strong impulse attraction for Kindle Store buyers. And this is as good a place as any for me to acknowledge that I was wrong to scoff, earlier this

year, at any author or publisher who would price a book below $2.99 under the new royalty structure. Although it is true that a 99-cent book would have to sell six times as many "copies" as a $2.99 book to achieve the same royalty earnings, it is clear to me that there are a significant number of books like L.J. Sellers' The Sex Club (http://amzn.to/sellersbook) and Scott Nicholson's Disintegration (http://amzn.to/nicholsonbook) whose sales are getting an extra boost in something like that 6:1 range because, in addition to being very good, highly rated reads, they also stand out due to their low prices.

5. **Overall eBook Prices Are Falling**. As much as we may be frustrated with the occasionally ridiculous individual price, and despite the last-gasp efforts of publishers who may be ensuring their own demise between the agency model scam and various other evidences of institutional cluelessness, there is a continuing trend toward reasonable ebook pricing that is evident in the Kindle Store prices. It is not a relentless downward spiral to zero, which would not serve any us well in the long run: the percentage of books priced below $2.99 has fallen dramatically since Amazon announced its new royalty structure. But the overall

percentage of books priced under $10, which was never over 80 percent prior to the agency model, grew to 84 percent by September 5 and stands at 85 percent today.

6. **Bestseller Prices are Also Falling Gradually**. While some big-name authors have been able to sustain high sales levels with prices at $12.99, $14.99 and even, in the case of Ken Follett, $19.99, the overall composition of the Top 100 Paid bestsellers in the Kindle Store continues to show a downward drift, with a high likelihood that even those books that hold on to Top 100 rankings at the higher agency model prices are leaving a lot of money on the table due to price resistance among price-conscious Kindle owners. As of this afternoon, only 26 of the top 100 were priced at $10 and up -- down from 30 in July and 28 in September -- and only three of those were priced above $12.99. Even the number of Top 100 bestsellers priced at $9.99 has taken a dive -- from 29 in September to 24 today -- so that *for the first time since Amazon began bifurcating its bestseller list to separate free listings from paid listings, fully half of the titles in the Top 100 Paid bestsellers are priced below $9.99*.

7. **Free Books are Still Getting the Love**. The number of free public domain books in the Kindle Store, which had held at just over 20,000 for over a year, dropped to about 16,550 when Amazon performed a bit of a housecleaning this Summer, and has held steady at the level for several months. There has been a gradual increase in the number of free contemporary or promotional titles in recent months, so that this figure as of this afternoon stood at 183, close to its highest level ever. Some of the promises of earlier this year, such as the one involving Amazon's collaboration with the British Library to release Kindle editions of over 60,000 free 19th century titles including the popular "penny dreadful" novels of that era, remain as far from being fulfilled as Google's monthly promise that it will launch Google Editions with a few months. And our hope that Amazon would level the playing field for indie authors be allowing the occasional indie-author freebie has, thus far at least, come to naught.

That's our story, and we're sticking to it. Here's a link that should bring up some of our past posts on pricing in the Kindle Store catalog (http://bit.ly/k-pricing).

17512189R00099

Made in the USA
Lexington, KY
13 September 2012